3.98

THE COMMUTER RAILROADS

COMMUTER RAILROADS

*A Pictorial Review of the
Most Travelled Railroads*

by

PATRICK C. DORIN

BONANZA BOOKS • NEW YORK

This edition published by Bonanza Books,
a division of Crown Publishers, Inc.
by arrangement with the Superior Publishing Company

a   b   c   d   e   f   g   h

PRINTED IN THE UNITED STATES OF AMERICA

*To the memory of my Father,
Aloysius Louis, and to my
Mother, Grace Margaret and
Brothers, Louis and William,
I dedicate this book.*

CONTENTS

INTRODUCTION 8

CHAPTER   I   Boston 13

CHAPTER   II New York
           New York State & Connecticut Service 31

CHAPTER III New York
           Long Island and New Jersey Service 42

CHAPTER IV Philadelphia 74

CHAPTER   V Washington-Baltimore, Pittsburgh and Cleveland 94

CHAPTER VI Chicago 103

CHAPTER VII San Francisco 155

CHAPTER VIII Montreal, Toronto and Detroit 164

APPENDIX 184

INDEX 191

AN INTERIOR VIEW of the Lake Street Chicago Transit Authority air conditioned rapid transit cars. An exterior view is shown in Chapter 5. The reader should compare this interior with the various interiors of suburban coaches throughout the book. This will illustrate the differences in the comfort index for the rapid transit intra city ride versus the longer city suburb ride on a Class I Railroad. (Courtesy Pullman Standard)

ANOTHER EXAMPLE is the Rapid Transit Service that has been expanded in the Philadelphia area. Here the first of the new Budd built rapid transit cars for Philadelphia areas Delaware River Port Authority completes a successful test along the 14½ mile right-of-way from Philadelphia to Lindenwold, New Jersey. The 80 seat semi-automated passenger cars are capable of 75 mph top speed. (Courtesy The Budd Company.)

Acknowledgments

Many people lent freely of their time and resources to this writer during the search for material for this book. For their time, assistance and encouragement, the author wishes to gratefully acknowledge the following people:

My wife Karen, who has sacrificed much of her time checking materials and reading and re-reading the manuscript for errors; my brother Louis Dorin for materials and photographs in Northern Indiana; Larry Leist for suburban railroad data and materials in the East; *The Gary Post Tribune;* and the following railroad photographers: Bob Lorenz, Franklin A. King, Jim Scribbins, Leonard Bachelder, Jack Dimond, and H. W. Pontin and others of the Rail Photo Service.

A special note of thanks must go to the following Operating and Public Relations men of the various Suburban Railroad and equipment manufacturers:

Baltimore and Ohio—D. A. Watts; Boston & Maine—G. F. Gallagher; Canadian National—J. C. Noel, A. Arseneau, R. A. Boden; Canadian Pacific—G. E. Benoit; Central Railroad Company of New Jersey—N. W. James; Chicago & North Western Railway—F. V. Koval, Thomas H. Smith; Burlington Route—A. M. Rung; Chicago, South Shore and South Bend Railroad—Railroad Consultants, Beveridge, Penney & Bennett, Inc. J. Petritz; Erie Lackawanna—G. W. Eastland; Government of Ontario Transit—E. A. Ingraham; Grand Trunk Western—H. F. MacLeod; Gulf, Mobile and Ohio—B. M. Sheridan; Illinois Central—C. G. Massoth; Long Island—E. K. Goldthwaite; Milwaukee Road—Marc Green; Norfolk and Western—John Ankenbruck; Penn Central—R. S. McKernan, R. L. McLean, Ann Kuss, H. L. Wiand, E. C. Rowell, T. J. Costello; Pennsylvania Reading Seashore Lines—H. L. Wiand; Pittsburgh and Lake Erie—R. R. Firestone; Reading Company—S. R. Spencer; Rock Island—J. G. Pate; Southern Pacific—R. A. Sederholm; Hawker Siddely Canada—W. F. Ogilvie; Canadian Vickers Limited—J. M. Pachman; Pullman Standard—E. Preston Calvert, John Sward, Jim Stillman, Don O'Barski; General Steel Industries—J. Dan House; Electro-Motive Division of General Motors—D. G. Cummings; Budd Company—P. O. Sichert; General Motors of Canada, Limited—G. Boyd Chesney.

Without the complete and unselfish cooperation of the above men and women, this book would not have been possible. Should an acknowledgment have been left out inadvertently, this writer trusts it will be found in its appropriate place within the book.

Introduction

The purpose of this book is to describe the Class I Railroad Suburban operations since the Depression and their plans for the future. Every week day, many railroad companies carry thousands of commuters to the business districts of New York City, Montreal, Chicago and other great cities in the morning and back home again in the evening. The railroad reaction to this service ranges from profitable delight to a deep deficit gloom. Moreover the service is extremely vital to the smooth flow of people in and out of our large cities. Therefore, in simple terms, it cannot die. Because of the increasing traffic snarls on our expressways, many states, provinces and cities are turning to the railroads for help. The government agencies are beginning to find out it is much cheaper to maintain adequate railroad service than it is to build and maintain highways.

Commuter Railroads are a top subject of conversation for many people. The commuter wonders if the service will be expanded, modernized or even abandoned. The rail fan favors the service to ride on and to watch the heavy density of traffic in those areas. The model railroader can find many ways of modeling and operating trains from the commuter service. Equipment varies from combination cars and coaches to club lounge and parlor cars, from diesel powered trains to electrics and Rail Diesel Cars, from one car scoots to 15 car rush hour limiteds. Some even have names,

ALTHOUGH IT IS NOT THE SCOPE of this book to cover Rail Rapid Transit Suburban Service (This area has been covered quite adequately during recent months by a number of very good authors.), this writer would like to point out a few differences between Class I Railroad Suburban Service and Rapid Transit.

First of all, each has a place in the transportation market. The Rapid Transit lines seem to be best for Intra-city transportation and perhaps out to the first line of surrounding suburbs. The equipment for this type of transportation is generally smaller and lighter than Class I Railroad equipment. Most of these cars are from 40 to 55 feet long. The longest equipment is the 69½ feet long cars operated by the Metropolitan Transit Authority of Boston on the 9 mile Cambridge-Dorchester line. These cars have a seating capacity of 56 and standing capacity of 266 passengers, and can attain a top speed of 55 mph. These cars are fine for distances of 10 or 12 miles where the ride is rather short in duration. But beyond that mile-

such as the "Morning Hotshot", "Cannon Ball" and "Banker's Special." One can find just about any type of passenger car or operation in commuter service as there is in long distance trains, except sleeping cars. Indeed, even long distance trains play a part in the suburban service; and sleeping cars have been used in commuter trains during equipment shortages. Although there is a wide variety of operations, all commuter operations have the same objective; to carry passengers safely to and from work.

Of the Millions of people that travel the city-suburb corridors every weekday, most of them drive instead of taking the train. People that are addicted to the driving habit claim they desire the privacy and convenience of their automobile—they can come and go as they please. However, the simple truth is that this is becoming less and less so. As our population expands, and more and more people are driving to and from the business districts of our large cities, traffic has slowed to a crawl on the expressways during the rush hours. Government officials and citizens all over the U. S. and Canada are wondering what can be done about it.

To solve this jumbo problem, we can either build new or expand the present expressway systems or we can set up new or expand the present railroad suburban service. The difficult question here is how to provide a balanced transportation system. Most of the large metropolitan areas are

age, it can be very tiresome to stand in crowded conditions for 40 minutes or more. The comfort index is good only for short distances.

Secondly, the suburban railroad train is heavier, and if equipped with modern equipment, much more comfortable for the longer distance ride of up to 40 miles for most suburbanites, and up to 100 for a few others. A modern double deck suburban coach can seat up to 169 passengers in air conditioned comfort. Therefore, it seems that the Class I Railroad is best for the longer distance commuter—and not for the intra city transportation that so many of the lines are providing today (1969). The ideal situation would be to have a few joint Railroad-City Rapid Transit stations within the city so that suburbanites could change from train to rapid transit at any point to travel to their destination—with single ticketing arrangement. The reverse should also hold true so that urban residents could travel easily to the outlying suburbs for the new employment opportunities that are growing in those areas. (Courtesy Pullman Standard)

presently engaged in extensive studies to determine how this can be done. The answers are going to be different for each area because of their individual differences and problems.

Both the expressway systems and the railroads have some very complex problems. To build or expand the present highway system, additional land has to be taken from residential and business areas. When the new expressway is completed, more automobiles will be on the roads, so more parking ramps have to be built in the down town area taking still more land away from the business section. It appears that the Super Expressway has reached the point of diminishing returns. Super Highways are extremely costly too, $3 to 6 million for building one mile of six lane highway. This figure varies according to geographic area. Labor and transportation costs of materials affect the price of construction also. The construction costs also zoom up to nearly $16 million per mile for elevated highways. With these costs, the alternative of building new expressways is becoming too expensive for the tax payers.

The railroads also have some very serious problems with their suburban business. At the present time, 22 railroad companies in the USA and Canada provide suburban service. For most of these companies, it is a great financial drain. There is only one commuter railroad that earns a profit without a subsidy. The basic reason, not the only one to be sure, is the peak rush hour traffic with a low volume of off hour traffic. The physical plant and equipment are in full use only 20 to 30 hours per week, very poor utilization to say the least. In addition, maintenance costs on older equipment are mounting year by year, and many of the lines cannot afford new equipment.

With the railroads and the highway systems facing these huge problems, the various states, provinces and cities are finding themselves in a serious transportation bind. To build new highways is almost futile, and the railroads cannot afford to expand or modernize their service by themselves. Yet a single track railroad can handle the same volume of passengers as a ten lane highway. So it appears that despite the railroads' commuter financial predicament, the commuter train is the most logical solution for the movement of people in the city-suburban corridors.

Economically, it is far less expensive to expand present or provide new railroad commuter service. For new service, the railroad plant is already in existence. For approximately $8 million, eight locomotives and about 50 single level coaches can be purchased. $8 million will barely build 2½ miles of expressway. The amount of equipment above can provide 30 minute off hour and 15 minute rush hour service over a 30 mile route. 30 miles of new expressway would cost $120 million. Note the wide difference in investment costs.

Private corporations could provide frequent suburban rail service. However, due to the peak traffic period and the use of a fare structure that would draw passengers from the expressway, they may not be able to earn a fair return on their investment. The railroads might be encouraged to expand their service by leasing and/or operating state owned equipment, tax relief or perhaps even a direct subsidy. By providing fast, frequent rail service, the highways could be relieved of some of the heavy traffic. Fast and frequent service would mean that the individual could go and come as he pleased—the very reason that many people drive their automobiles. If more people were riding suburban trains, less highways and parking ramps would have to be built, and this would be much less expensive for the tax payers.

Many communities are adopting the above logic and are providing assistance to the railroads, and are expanding their rapid transit systems. One could say that at no time in the History of American Railroading has there been a greater challenge in the transportation of passengers as there is today.

PATRICK C. DORIN

Duluth, Minnesota
August 1, 1969

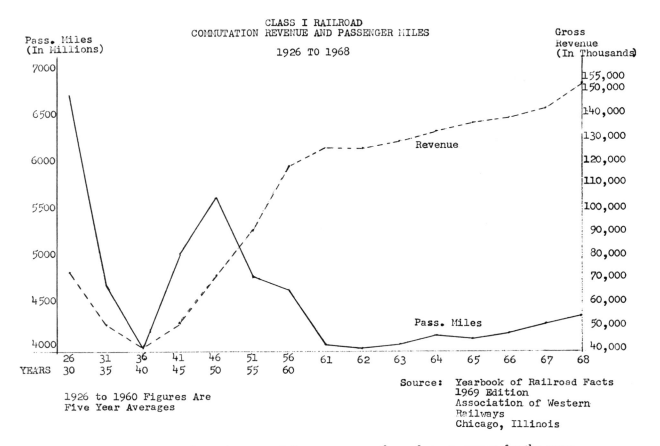

Pass. Miles
(In Millions)

Gross
Revenue
(In Thousands)

1926 to 1960 Figures Are
Five Year Averages

Source: Yearbook of Railroad Facts
          1969 Edition
          Association of Western
          Railways
          Chicago, Illinois

THE ABOVE GRAPH shows the commutation passenger miles and gross revenue for the years just prior to the depression through to 1968. The revenue figure has been setting a new record every year since 1949 despite the continued decline in traffic until bottoming out in 1962. The reason for this, of course, has been extensive fare increases; yet commutation fares are still very much a bargain in this period of rapid inflation. The suburbanite pays less than an average of 3.75¢ per mile for his monthly ticket.

Since 1926, suburban traffic has had two periods of rapid decline in business. The first, through 1936, was due primarily to the depression. The second, beginning after World War II, was due to the increase in number of private automobiles and the reduction of the six day work week to five days. The latter alone accounted for over a 15% loss in commuter traffic.

There is also a third reason for the over all loss of business in the National Picture. Shortly after World War II and through the early 1950's, many Class I lines discontinued or greatly reduced their suburban operations. The Pacific Electric (Los Angeles) and the Northwestern Pacific (San Francisco-Oakland Area) are two examples of large operations being discontinued entirely. Many other railroads, such as the Missouri Pacific and Louisville & Nashville had minor suburban services that have been discontinued.

During the 1920's, many cities and towns throughout the United States and Canada supported commuter services of various magnitudes. An example is the Omaha Railroad's commuter service between Ashland, Wisconsin (In 1920, Ashland's population was over 20,000), Washburn and a DuPont Plant located between the two cities. The operation consisted of 33 daily trains. The Milwaukee Road also operated commuter trains to various coal mines in Southern Indiana. Nearly all of these services died in the late 1920's and early 30's. It was a combination of all these factors that led to the nearly 40% drop in the total National Commuter Passenger Miles in the ten year period from 1926 to 1936. The War brought a slight come back, but the automobile nearly finished it off during the fifteen years after the War.

Since 1962, the commuter passenger miles have been increasing. However, except on a few lines such as the Chicago & North Western, this increase is actually a heavy increase in rush hour traffic with a continued decline in off peak hour service. This condition has placed an even more difficult strain for some railroad's abilities to continue to provide such service. It is easy to see that if a large fleet of equipment, tracks and stations are used only 20 hours per week that it would be difficult to earn a return on the stockholders' investment. The increase in business since 1962 is due to over crowded super highways.

Above graph is for U.S.A. only and does not include Canadian Statistics.

AN EXAMPLE OF Governmental Assistance to the railroads for Suburban Train Operations and Improvements is the following Chart of Improvements for Northern New Jersey. (Courtesy Central Railroad of New Jersey)

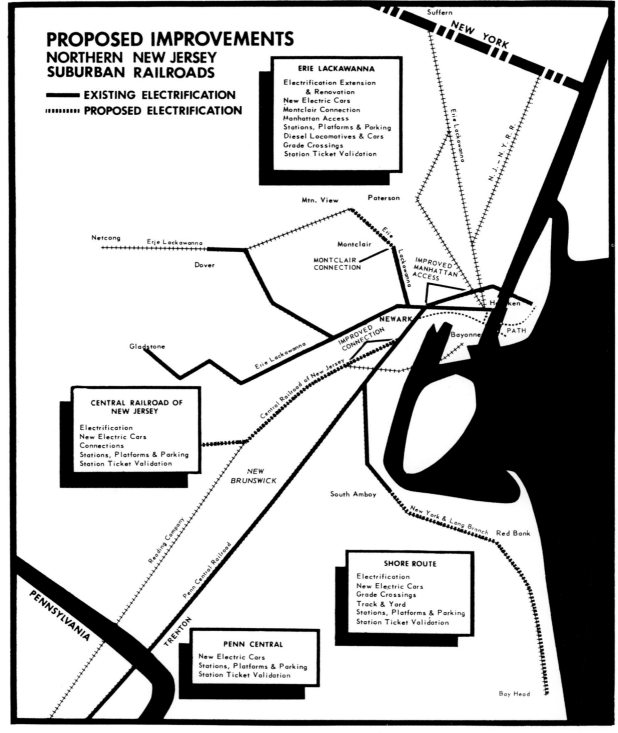

PROPOSED IMPROVEMENTS
NORTHERN NEW JERSEY
SUBURBAN RAILROADS

━━━ **EXISTING ELECTRIFICATION**
▪▪▪▪▪▪▪ **PROPOSED ELECTRIFICATION**

ERIE LACKAWANNA

Electrification Extension
  & Renovation
New Electric Cars
Montclair Connection
Manhattan Access
Stations, Platforms & Parking
Diesel Locomotives & Cars
Grade Crossings
Station Ticket Validation

CENTRAL RAILROAD OF NEW JERSEY

Electrification
New Electric Cars
Connections
Stations, Platforms & Parking
Station Ticket Validation

SHORE ROUTE

Electrification
New Electric Cars
Grade Crossings
Track & Yard
Stations, Platforms & Parking
Station Ticket Validation

PENN CENTRAL

New Electric Cars
Stations, Platforms & Parking
Station Ticket Validation

Suffern
NEW YORK
N. J. - N. Y. R. R.
Erie Lackawanna
Paterson
Mtn. View
Netcong
Erie Lackawanna
Montclair
MONTCLAIR CONNECTION
Dover
Erie Lackawanna
IMPROVED MANHATTAN ACCESS
Hoboken
PATH
Bayonne
NEWARK
IMPROVED CONNECTION
Gladstone
Erie Lackawanna
Central Railroad of New Jersey
NEW BRUNSWICK
South Amboy
New York & Long Branch
Red Bank
Reading Company
Penn Central Railroad
PENNSYLVANIA
TRENTON
Bay Head

Chapter 1

BOSTON

Boston and Maine Corporation

The Boston and Maine Railroad operates a Suburban Service over four different routes plus four branches radiating North and West of Boston. The Company carries over 24,000 week day passengers on 236 trains that arrive and depart North Station. However, the volume of passengers and trains has a deceivingly profitable look to it.

A few years ago, the B&M applied to the ICC for permission to discontinue all passenger service. This permission was granted and all long distance train service was discontinued. The commutation service was continued through a contract with the Massachusetts Bay Transportation Authority. This agreement provides that the B&M operate the service and bill the MBTA for the operating deficit. In this case, the annual loss is approximately $3.2 million. At this time (1969) there is considerable thought being given to the plan of the MBTA purchasing all passenger equipment from the Boston and Maine. As yet, no decision has been reached.

The B&M train operations are fairly simple in that all trains are made up of Budd RDC's and there is no need for switching or turning of equipment. The Budd Cars are set up in a pool that provides that 86 cars are used to operate 236 weekday trains of one to eight cars in length. The following table describes the train service on the various lines into and out of Boston.

SUBURBAN TERMINAL MILEAGE FROM BOSTON

Terminal	Mileage
Rockport	35.3
Ipswich	27.7
Reading	12.0
Woburn	10.0
Lowell	25.3
Ayer	36.0
South Sudbury	19.7
Bedford	14.8
Haverhill	33.3
Newburyport	37.2

Train service frequency varies from one route to another. On the Woburn-Lowell route, the frequency varies from 30 to 60 minutes to those destinations. Also service is staggered to give 15 minute headways during rush hours between Boston and Winchester. On week ends this service is reduced to one hour frequencies on Saturdays and up to three hour frequencies on Sundays and Holidays.

On the Ipswich-Rockport lines, weekday service is staggered between the two lines to give 20 minute peak hour service and one hour non rush service between Boston and Beverly. Beverly is the junction for the two lines. Week-end service is reduced to approximately every two hours on Saturdays and every three hours on Sundays and Holidays.

SUBURBAN TRAIN SERVICE FREQUENCY

Between Boston and	Week Days				Sat.		Sun.	
	Total Train Serv. AR. BOST	LV. BOST	A.M. Rush Hour AR. BOST	P.M. Rush Hour LV. BOST	AR. BOST	LV. BOST	AR. BOST	LV. BOST
Woburn-Lowell	37	38	10	11	22	22	13	13
Ipswich and Rockport	27	28	9	9	17	17	11	11
Ayer	19	19	6	5	8	8	4	4
Reading	31	29	12	9	17	17	15	15
South Sudbury	1	1	1	1	0	0	0	0
Bedford	1	1	1	1	0	0	0	0
Haverhill	1	1	1	1	0	0	0	0
Newburyport	1	1	1	1	0	0	0	0
Total	118	118	41	38	64	64	43	43

On the West Concord line, week day service is approximately hourly. Only two trains operate to and from Ayer. Saturday service varies from 2 to 5 hours and there are but four trains in each direction on Sunday.

The Boston-Reading service is approximately every 60 minutes on both week days and week ends.

There is no mid day, evening, or week end service on the South Sudbury, Haverhill, Bedford, Beaverbrook or the Newburyport lines.

In order to provide this service, the B&M relies solely on a fleet of 86 Budd RDC cars. The company owns 44 RDC-1's, 13 RDC-2's, 6 RDC-3's and 23 RDC-9's. The RDC-9 is a full coach with only half the power of a standard RDC and is not equipped with train controls.

The Boston and Maine has a large number of trains, yet they carry only 24,000 week day passengers. Most of these passengers use the usual morning and evening rush hour service. The service has been a serious financial drain on the B&M because of the low number of non rush hour passengers and the resulting poor utilization of equipment. The MBTA subsidy has kept 24,000 passengers off the highways and the result has been a savings to the public in the form of less highway construction and maintenance. The present MBTA contract extends only to the end of July, 1969. With this contract, the B&M is not losing any money on the service, but the stock holders are not making any return on their investments. The present situation, clearly, cannot continue. The State will either have to take over the service completely, and take it off the Railroad's hands—or it may be abandoned completely, a very poor alternative to say the least.

The State Legislature has ordered the MBTA to come up with a Master Plan for commuter service. This plan should include the present or extension of the rapid transit service, the retention or the rejection of the present B&M rail service, and additional rail or bus service. At this time, it is not known what this Master Plan will be, and no doubt it will be changed several times after it is set up. One thing is certain however, the B&M's 24,000 week day passengers can hardly be handled on buses. Some form of Rail Transportation is the only logical solution to this Boston Suburban Service crisis.

AN EVENING PORTRAIT of commuter rush hour runs behind Boston & Maine Pacific type steam locomotives at North Station, Boston in 1941. (Courtesy Chris Lazos, Rail Photo Service)

DURING THE DAYS OF STEAM, The Boston & Maine powered their suburban trains with Pacific type steam locomotives, such as the No. 3622 pictured here at Boston between runs in 1953. In 1955, there were but 8 passenger steam locomotives and 5 dual purpose engines left on the property. Diesel road switchers replaced most of the steam power in suburban service prior to the purchase of Rail Diesel Cars. (Courtesy Bob Lorenz)

UP UNTIL the early 1950's, doodlebugs were used in non rush hour suburban service by the Boston and Maine. This Gas-electric with trailer is departing North Station for Manchester, Mass. in the Spring of 1952. (Courtesy W. G. Fancher, Rail Photo Service)

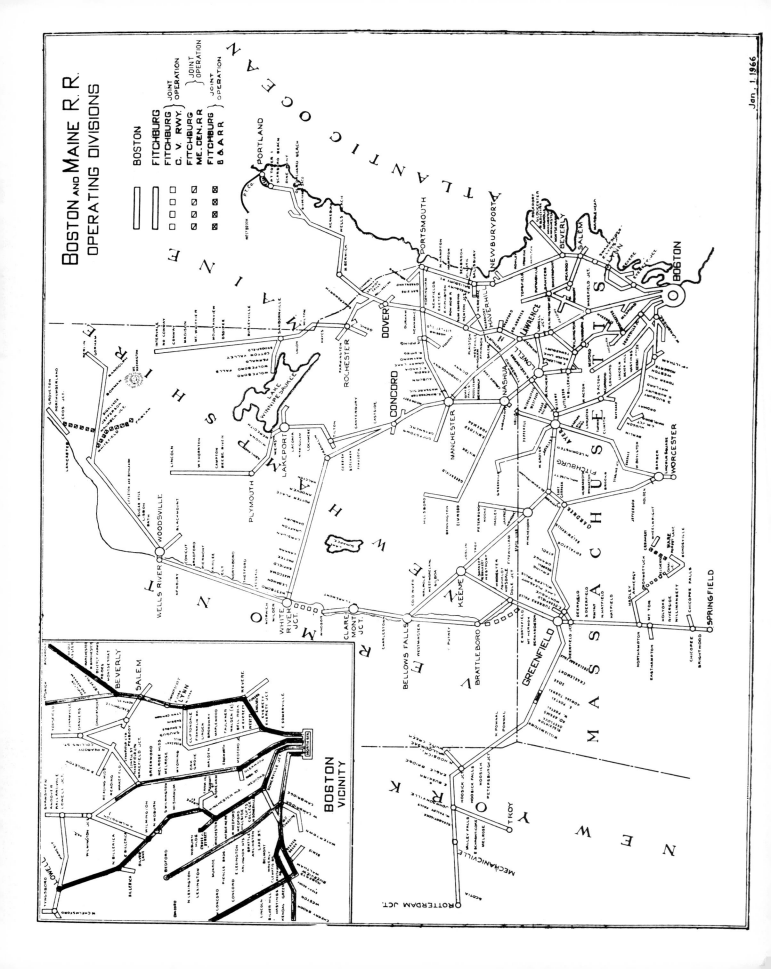

BOSTON AND MAINE R.R. OPERATING DIVISIONS

Jan. 1, 1966

BOSTON

FITCHBURG

FITCHBURG
C. V. RWY. } JOINT OPERATION

FITCHBURG
ME. CEN. R.R. } JOINT OPERATION

FITCHBURG
B & A.R.R } JOINT OPERATION

BOSTON VICINITY

AT THE PRESENT TIME, the B&M owns 6 RDC-3's. These cars are used in suburban service along with all other Boston & Maine Rail Diesel Cars. (Courtesy the Budd Company)

ALL BOSTON & MAIN suburban service is run under contract to the Massachusetts Bay Transportation Authority, whose legal boundaries encompass the Census Bureaus "Standard Metropolitan Area" plus the town of Maynard. In terms of B&M lines, this means Manchester, Hamilton, Reading, Wilmington, Woburn, Bedford, West Concord and South Sudbury. Some towns outside the district have entered into contracts with the MBTA for service on the basis of making up the difference between fares collected and the extra cost of running to their town.

This photo shows B&M train No. 1222 on a Saturday at Ipswich. Normally Saturday traffic requires only one car trains. However, in this case an extra car has been added to the train for a special party. (Courtesy J. Leonard Bachelder)

MANY BOSTON & MAINE passenger trains performed suburban service as their prime passenger function, but did not terminate within the defined suburban territory. An example of this was the Boston-Nashua train. Nashua is located 39.0 miles out of Boston on the Concord Line. This train not only provided suburban service, but also provided local service and mail, express and milk service into the State of New Hampshire. The train, as shown along the banks of the Merrimac River, has now of course been discontinued since this photo was taken in 1950. Prior to the use of RDC's, the B&M employed road switchers in suburban service. (Courtesy S. K. Bolton, Jr. Rail Photo Service)

AN INTERIOR VIEW of a Boston & Maine RDC-1. RDC-1's have a seating capacity of 90 seats and those operating in suburban service were generally equipped with "walk over" seats, such as shown here or "flip over" seats. All RDC's were equipped with baggage racks extending the entire length of the car. Lighting was provided by both over the seat and over the center aisle lights. The interior of an RDC-9 is identical to a RDC-1. The interiors of the 2's and 3's are also similar except that they have smaller passenger compartments, and hence a seating capacity of 71 and 49 respectively. (Courtesy Jim Scribbins)

THREE CAR RDC train, including an RDC-3, No. 2215 departing North Station for Haverhill, Mass. (Courtesy W. G. Fancher, Rail Photo Service)

BOSTON & MAIN RDC-1 heads into a late Saturday afternoon Sun leaving the Boston North Station. Is the conductor watching for late comers who might be chasing the train? Note the automatic car identification strip on the left end of the car. (Courtesy Jim Scribbins)

THE ONLY PLACE one can purchase a ticket now (1969) on the B&M (besides on the trains) is at Boston. All stations are now either boarded up—as shown here—torn down or converted to some other use. This is a typical right of way scene. The station is at South Acton. (Courtesy J. Leonard Bachelder)

RUSH HOUR TRAIN No. 108 en route to Boston with one RDC-2 and four RDC-1's. This train originated at Haverhill and rush hour service only is provided on the line. RDC-2's and 3's are used in suburban service, even though there is no mail or baggage service, simply because there are not enough RDC-1's to go around. (Courtesy J. Leonard Bachelder)

IT TAKES quite a fleet of RDC equipment to serve the heavy traffic of the Rockport Line (North Shore Area). This scene shows a small portion of the number required at the Rockport yard. Although the station has been retired, the train service in 1969 is more frequent than it was ten years ago. The blind end car is an RDC-9—no controls, with only one engine and intended to run between 2 standard RDC's. The B&M once owned 30 such cars. Now many of the RDC-9's have been sold to the Canadian National. (Courtesy J. Leonard Bachelder)

A **FOUR CAR** rush hour suburban RDC train on the Boston and Maine at Boston not far from North Station. The B&M also operated RDC's extensively on most of their through train operations during the last years of such service. Most of the B&M through train operations were rather short. For example, the mileage between Boston and Portland, Maine is only 115.0 miles, shorter by 2.4 miles than the 117.4 mile New York-Montauk Long Island Railroad suburban run. (Courtesy W. G. Fancher, Rail Photo Service)

The Penn Central Company

The Penn Central operates a limited suburban passenger service in the Boston area over five lines, that radiate from the west to the southwest of that great city.

Suburban trains are operated over the main line of the former Boston and Albany Railroad; and over four other lines of the former New Haven Railroad, which is now known as the New Haven Region. The railroad carries a total of 5500 week day passengers on 92 week day trains. The Company is experiencing a loss on the operations, but part of the service is covered by a financial reimbursement contract with the Massachusetts Bay Transportation Authority similar to the agreement covering the Boston and Maine train service.

The first line mentioned above runs west on the former B&A from Boston to Framingham and Worcester, a distance of 44.3 miles. This line is served by 3 inbound and 3 outbound rush hour trains, which arrive at South Station, Boston between 8:00 A.M. and 8:40 A.M. and depart between 4:45 P.M. and 5:45 P.M. Four of the six commuter trains originate and terminate at Framingham instead of Worcester. The former "New England States" also operates over this line and provides additional train service by stopping at Back Bay Station, Newtonville, Framingham and Worcester. Todays service on the exB&A is but a small fraction of

a once extensive commuter service over not only the main line, but over a number of the short branches in the Boston area. Some of this close in trackage is now served by Rapid Transit Service.

The next line extends west-southwest from Boston to Needham Heights, a distance of 14.0 miles. At the present time, week day service sees 11 trains to Boston and 12 to suburbia on this line. There are four rush hour arrivals between 7:30 A.M. and 9:00 A.M., and five departures between 4:00 P.M. and 6:00 P.M. at Boston. Week day service begins at 6:50 A.M. and continues until nearly 10:00 P.M. Off hour train service ranges from 1 to 4½ hours apart, with most of the service to Boston before noon; and from Boston after 2:00 P.M. Saturday service sees 6 trains to Boston and 5 from Boston. All trains on this line are equipped with Rail Diesel Cars. The Needham service is provided through contract with the M.T.B.A.

The third suburban territory is actually a branch off of the Boston-New York main line and it extends to the southwest of Boston to Franklin, a distance of 28.0 miles. Week day sees 6 arrivals at Boston from the Franklin line, and 7 departures to suburbia. Not all of these trains originate or terminate at Franklin. One eastbound and one westbound originate and terminate at Walpole, while another pair of trains operate in the same manner to and from Norwood Central. All other trains operate between Franklin

DURING THE DAYS of steam, the Boston and Albany operated the World's largest Tank Passenger Steam Locomotives. This commuter train is arriving at Riverside in 1939 with one of the five super passenger tanks, the 401. (Courtesy H. W. Pontin, Rail Photo Service)

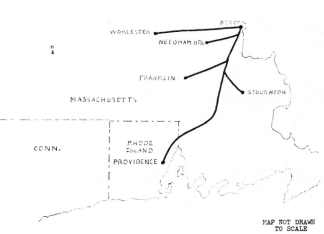

PENN CENTRAL COMPANY
BOSTON SUBURBAN TERRITORY

WORCESTER
NEEDHAM HTS.
FRANKLIN
MASSACHUSETTS
STOUGHTON
BOSTON
CONN.
RHODE ISLAND
PROVIDENCE

MAP NOT DRAWN TO SCALE

VIEW FROM TERMINAL TOWER in July, 1950 with suburban train arriving at Boston's South Station from the Milford Branch. (Courtesy W. G. Fancher, Rail Photo Service)

FOUR NEW YORK CENTRAL (Boston & Albany Lines) locals are ready to depart for Boston Suburbia from Boston's South Station Terminal. The Hudson, No. 601, was making its last trip to Springfield, Mass. The three other locals were already diesel powered as the photo was taken in 1950. (Courtesy H. W. Pontin, Rail Photo Service)

and Boston. Of the total service, 3 eastbounds arrive Boston between 7:00 A.M. and 9:00 A.M., and three westbounds depart Boston between 4:00 P.M. and 6:00 P.M. Saturday service consists of three trains in each direction. There is no train service on Sunday.

Off hour trains on the Franklin line are equipped with RDC's and rush hour trains are equipped with standard coaches and diesel powered.

The Franklin service is also under contract with the M.B.T.A.

The next territory is the busy Boston-Providence local service. Providence is 44.0 miles south-south-west of Boston, and is on the New York-Boston main line. This territory is served by through New York-Boston streamliners and by suburban runs. The line is quite busy with 20 eastbound and 19 westbound week day trains. The 7:00 A.M. to 9:00 A.M. rush hour period sees 5 arrivals at Boston. The 4:00 P.M. to 6:00 P.M. has 6 departures to Suburbia. All but one train in each direction operate between Boston and Providence. This exception is a rush hour train to Readsville, which returns immediately to Boston upon discharging passengers.

Non rush hour service is approximately every 60 minutes or oftener. Service begins before 6:00 A.M. and the last train departs Boston at 10:00 P.M. Saturday service sees 15 trains in each direction. There are 11 eastbounds and 10 westbounds on Sunday.

THE FORMER New Haven used a variety of steam power in suburban service on the Boston-Providence Line including Atlantics and Type I Pacifics. This power headed up both expresses and locals between Boston and Providence, and in the other Boston Suburban Territories. Equipment during the 30's and 40's was much the same as it is now, both standard and streamlined. New Haven Atlantic type No. 1107 is heading toward Boston with a non stop express made up of two streamlined coaches. (Courtesy H. W. Pontin, Rail Photo Service)

LIMA-HAMILTON unit with eastbound commuter local from Framingham (21 miles out) passing Tower 6, Huntington Avenue, Boston. The standard Boston & Albany and New York Central equipment shown at the right of the photo is still used in Penn Central Boston-Worcester service today. The Lima Hamiltons and Alcos, however, have been replaced with black Penn Central E units. Also, today (1969) there are but three suburban trains in each direction compared with five trains in each direction in 1966, and nearly hourly service on the main line and several branches thirty years ago. Part of the right of way of former B&A suburban service is now part of Boston's Rapid Transit System. (Courtesy S. K. Bolton, Jr., Rail Photo Service)

A SINGLE RDC-1 is able to handle all the off peak and Saturday service on the Needham Branch. This is train No. 958 at Needham Heights. (Courtesy J. Leonard Bachelder)

THE SMALL EASTBOUND SHELTER at the new Route 128 station (The station itself is on the westbound side just out of the picture to the left.) and the Route 128 bridge form a backdrop for the RDC 1 No. 43 eastbound as train No. 556. The railroad guard is standing on the crossing to warn people who might try to cross that a westbound train is approaching. There are also red lights flashing and bell ringing for additional warning. RDC's serve certain non rush hour runs on the Providence locals, although most of the service is with standard equipment. (Courtesy J. Leonard Bachelder)

The suburban trains are equipped with either RDC's or are conventional trains with both standard and/or streamlined coaches. As some suburban equipment is used in both the Boston and New York areas, the roster of New Haven Region equipment is included in the chapter on New York City.

The last line is a four mile branch off the New York-Boston line. This is the line to Stoughton from Canton Junction. Stoughton is 19.0 miles from Boston. The operation here is quite simple. RDC's handle two week day rush hour trains to Boston in the morning, and to Stoughton in the evening. Saturday service consists of one train in each direction, with no service on Sunday.

Although most of the Boston service is now operating at a loss, the operation is providing all weather transportation for thousands of people in that area. If the Boston service were to be shut down completely, it would be almost impossible for one to drive to or from Boston with any time efficiency. Fortunately, local and state governments are beginning to recognize the value of the Penn Central's Boston Suburban Service.

INCLUDED IN THE LAST ORDER of standard Budd Rail Diesel Cars in 1953 were 3 RDC-4's. Although these cars were not used for suburban service, they are now out of service and are being cannibalized for parts for RDC's used in commuter operations. (Courtesy The Budd Company)

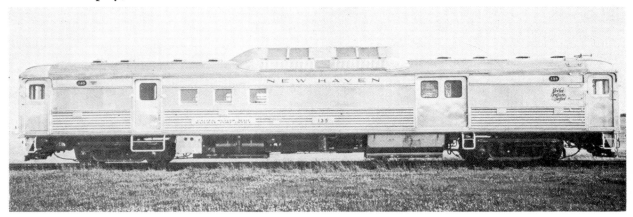

THROUGH TRAINS between New York and Boston handle a number of commuters between New London and Providence to Boston. These diesel powered trains take some of the pressure off the crowded rush hour commuter trains on the east end of the New Haven Region of the Penn Central Company. (Courtesy Bob Lorenz)

AN EX-NEW HAVEN suburban train No. 931 for Needham Heights passing through Forest Hills behind an Alco passenger unit 0704, type DL-109, Otto Kuhler style. These units were employed in passenger service during the day and freight service at night, a very successful operation for the New Haven. All these units have now been scrapped. (Courtesy S. K. Bolton, Jr., Rail Photo Service)

NEW HAVEN suburban train No. 555 with Alco No. 549 crossing the famous Canton Viaduct. (Courtesy S. K. Bolton, Jr., Rail Photo Service)

THE STANDARD consist of many ex New Haven suburban trains in 1969 is a Geep with as many coaches as are required for the particular run. New Haven GP-9 No. 7535 is shown here prior to departure from Boston South Station with a rush hour run to Providence. (Courtesy Carl H. Smith)

THE PENN CENTRAL is still operating the last of the 1950 light weight experiments, the modified and streamlined RDC's, "The Roger Williams." The equipment is presently operated with standard RDC's in Boston area suburban service. The Roger Williams is also equipped for third rail electric operation, which means the train could be operated in the New York third rail territory. (Courtesy Carl H. Smith)

THE MERCHANTS LIMITED at South Station prior to departure for New York City. This train is equipped with dining and lounge facilities as well as parlor cars and coaches, and provides commuter businessmen with an afternoon departure to New York City. (Courtesy Carl H. Smith)

Chapter 2

NEW YORK

New York State and Connecticut Service

The Penn Central Company

The Penn Central's New York State and Connecticut suburban service is one of the most extensive operation of trains to be found anywhere. The Grand Central Terminal at New York is certainly one of the busiest railroad stations in the world with 216 inbound and 215 outbound suburban trains every week day. These 431 trains carry 140 thousand passengers every weekday.

The suburban district is actually divided into two districts or regions. One is the New Haven Region between Grand Central and New Haven, a distance of 72.5 miles. This route also includes the New Canaan Branch, which leaves the main line at Stamford. The distance between Stamford and New Canaan is 7.5 miles. New Canaan itself is 41.0 miles northeast of New York City.

The other district is the former New York Central's Hudson and Harlem Divisions, which operate north and north northeast of New York City. The Hudson Division extends north along the Hudson River to Poughkeepsie, a distance of 72 miles. The Harlem Division first extends northeast and then north to Brewster, a distance of 52 miles.

The New York State and Connecticut service has several different types of operating procedures and trains. There are two types of electrified territory: third rail and overhead wire. Equipment consists of several types of MU electric coaches and standard and streamlined coaches. Rail Diesel Cars are also used on two of the three routes. Conventional trains are powered by both third rail and overhead wire electric locomotives, standard diesel power beyond electrified territory, and by diesel locomotives that are equipped for third rail electric operation into Grand Central Terminal. Here is railroading with many different flavors.

The line to Brewster, the Harlem Division, is the busiest of the three lines. Service on this route is continuous throughout the 24 hour day. The off hour frequency varies from 15 to 30 minutes during the day and evening to hourly from 1:00 A.M. to 5:00 A.M. There are a total of 81 arrivals at Grand Central from this line, and 85 departures to subur-

bia. Grand Central sees 48 departures and 47 arrivals on Saturday, and 45 each way on Sunday.

Rush hour service between 6:30 A.M. and 9:00 A.M. sees 23 arrivals at Grand Central. From 4:00 P.M. to 6:30 P.M., there are 30 departures. Therefore, the rush hour service consists of about one third of the total weekday service. The week end service is essentially the same as week days, with the deletion of most of the rush hour trains.

Most of the trains originate and terminate at White Plains, the present limit of third rail electrified territory. Of the total number of weekday trains, only 24 terminate at Brewster, while 20 originate at that point. Brewster service begins after 5:30 A.M. and continues until 1:00 A.M.

The Hudson Division (to Harmon and Poughkeepsie) is the other former New York Central suburban territory. This line, though quite busy, has the least amount of suburban traffic of the three lines. It is also the PC's main line to Chicago. Week day service sees 64 departures and 58 arrivals at Grand Central, with an off hour train service frequency of 15 to 30 minutes. The rush hour service consists of 22 departures between 4:00 P.M. and 6:30 P.M.; and 18 arrivals between 6:30 A.M. and 9:00 A.M. The rush hour service makes up about one third of the total week day service. Week-end service consists of 30 trains in each direction on Saturday, and 28 each way Sunday.

The Hudson Division operation could be split into two categories: Trains between Croton-Harmon and Grand Central (third rail electrified territory), and trains between Croton-Harmon and Poughkeepsie. Most of the train service mentioned above operates between Grand Central and Croton-Harmon. For service beyond Croton-Harmon, there are 21 northbound and 20 southbound connecting trains that operate between that point and Peekskill. Over one half of these trains operate beyond to Poughkeepsie. All of these trains connect directly with Grand Central-Croton-Harmon trains. This type of operation is known as Zone Scheduling, and in this case, it eliminates the motive power change at Croton-Harmon. There are, however, two trains in each direction that are through New York City-

Poughkeepsie runs. These four trains change from electric to diesel power or vice versa depending upon direction of travel at Croton-Harmon.

The equipment used on the Hudson and Harlem Division trains is drawn from a suburban passenger car pool. The connecting trains on the Hudson Division are equipped with RDC's and standard and streamlined coaches with conventional diesel power. Trains between New York City and Croton-Harmon and also to White Plains on the Harlem Division are equipped with electric locomotives and either standard and/or streamlined coaches. Trains in the electrified territories are also equipped with electric MU coaches. Rail Diesel cars are used between all points. When in electrified territory, the RDC's are pulled by either electric locomotives or by the MU coaches. The amount of equipment used on these two lines is broken down as follows:

Electric Multiple Unit Club Car	1
Electric Multiple Unit Coaches	234
Rail Diesel Cars	19
Streamlined Coaches	40
Standard Coaches	110

The Harlem and Hudson Divisions have been experiencing increases in both rush hour and non rush hour traffic in the past few years. This has resulted in the addition of both off hour trains and week end trains on both lines. The Zone Scheduling mentioned above enabled the PC to improve the utilization of its suburban fleet while handling an increase in business. This meant that the PC did not have to put additional cars into suburban service for the new business. This increase in business, and the public assistance plans have given the Hudson and Harlem Divisions a new lease on life, and they now have a brighter looking future.

ELECTRIFICATION CAME to the New York Central as a result of a serious accident in the Park Avenue tunnel approach to the Grand Central Station in 1902. The State Legislature then ordered the abandonment of steam operations in the tunnel by 1908.

General Electric built the **prototype third** rail electric steeplecab locomotive and road tested it in 1904. From that time, **it took** the New York Central Railroad nearly 10 years to completely electrify its present **routes**. The GE electric locomotive No. 110 is very similar to the original 86 ton locomotive **built in 1904**. These locomotives are no longer used in suburban service, but a few still **see some** yard service. (Courtesy Bob Lorenz)

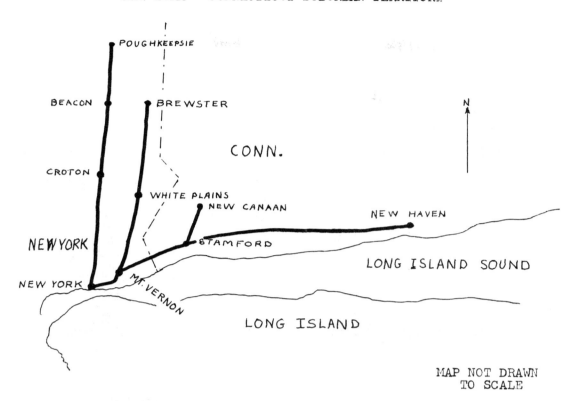

MAP NOT DRAWN
TO SCALE

The Penn Central's New Haven Region serves the Connecticut suburbs between New Haven and New York City. This suburban district is not quite as busy as the Harlem Division. With 67 eastbound and 76 westbound trains every week day. This number includes both suburban trains and through trains to Stamford, New Canaan, New Haven and beyond. New Haven Region through trains handle a considerable amount of suburban territory business. Not all of the trains mentioned above operate as far as New Haven. Many of these originate or terminate at Stamford. Week end service sees 48 departures and 41 arrivals at Grand Central on Saturday, and 38 departures and 40 arrivals on Sunday.

As mentioned previously, the New Canaan branch leaves the main line at Stamford. Service on this line consists of a shuttle service between Stamford and New Canaan. There are 18 trains in each direction on weekdays, while week end service sees 13 and 8 each way on Saturday and Sunday respectively. Passengers to and from the New Canaan branch must change trains at Stamford, except for passengers on the two through New York–New Canaan trains that are operated in each direction during the rush hours. The entire line between New York City and New Haven, including the New Canaan Branch is electrified with overhead wire.

Most of the suburban trains in this territory are equipped with electric MU coaches. However, a number of trains are equipped with standard and/or streamlined coaches and are powered by electric locomotives. Many of the through trains in this territory are diesel powered with EMD Dual-power third-rail locomotives, known as FL-9's. This operating procedure permits through Boston-New York locomotive assignments, and the FL-9 draws power from third rail while running on Grand Central Terminal trackage.

As mentioned in the chapter on Boston, some of the suburban equipment is often used in either New York or Boston service. Indeed, almost the entire New Haven Region could be considered a suburban railroad. Therefore, the following roster of equipment used in suburban service also indicates if the cars are used exclusively in one area or in both areas.

Type	Number	Location
Electric MU Standard Coaches	32	New York
Electric MU Streamlined Coaches	98	New York
Electric MU Trailers	54	New York
Electric MU Bar Cars	5	New York
Rail Diesel Cars	35	Boston
Standard Coaches	24	Both*
Streamlined Coaches	113	Both*

* Used primarily in New York—New Haven and Boston—Providence trains. Therefore, these cars frequently get shifted from one end of the New Haven Region to the other.

MULTIPLE UNIT electric coach service was inaugurated in 1905 and extended throughout the entire electrified territory in 1914. Service was provided by some 200 coaches similar or identical to the No. 4077. These original cars are no longer in service on the former New York Central Lines. (Courtesy Bob Lorenz)

The New Haven Region is part of the Main Line of the Northeast Corridor. A visitor from that area recently remarked to this writer that highway travel is becoming next to impossible. It is readily apparent that the railroad and the highway are needed together for a balanced transportation system. There is no such balance in the East today. However, state and local authorities are recognizing this situation, particularly since highways are now at or near their full capacity. The result has been public assistance plans which have cut the Penn Central's suburban deficits. Since the railroad is the only all weather transportation, and is the safest mode of travel; the railroad must be part of a balanced transportation system. Because of this fact, and recent state and local government action, the New York State and Connecticut suburban service can now be viewed with much more optimism.

STANDARD MULTIPLE UNIT commuter train at High Bridge station in 1939. Much of this equipment has been replaced by streamlined MU equipment. (Courtesy H. W. Clauson, Rail Photo Service)

AN EX CLEVELAND Union Terminal electric locomotive between runs at the White Plains, New York yard. (Courtesy Bob Lorenz)

ELECTRIC LOCOMOTIVE NO. 271 with a suburban train at White Plains, New York. White Plains is an important suburban train terminal on the former New York Central. (Courtesy Bob Lorenz)

PRIOR TO DIESELIZATION, the New York Central operated their suburban trains north of the electrified territory with light and average weight steam power. Here the 4675, a "Pacific" has arrived at the Poughkeepsie, New York station with a suburban train consisting of standard coaches. The time is 1947 and scenes such as this one were soon to be gone forever.

Poughkeepsie is an important suburban terminal with quite a few trains originating and terminating at that point. Poughkeepsie is 73.6 miles north of New York City on the New York to Buffalo Main Line of the Hudson Division. (Courtesy Bob Lorenz)

TWO PULLMAN STANDARD streamlined electric MU coaches make up the consist of ex-New York Central Hudson Division commuter train #735 near Ossining, New York. The train is passing through the shadows of the famed Sing Sing prison guard towers on its northbound run to Crotan-Harmon. (Courtesy J. W. Swanberg)

IN THE FORMER New York Central non electrified territory, commuter trains north of Harmon or White Plains are either diesel powered or equipped with Rail Diesel Cars, such as the M-451 shown here. (Courtesy W. G. Fancher, Rail Photo Service)

ELECTRIC SERVICE on the New Haven Railroad began in 1907 between New York and New Rochelle. During that year, suburban service was extended all the way to Stamford; but complete electrification of present lines was not completed until 1914. Original electric service was handled by Baldwin-Westinghouse locomotives. By 1909 however, open end electric MU coaches arrived on the property. This type of equipment was operated until the 1950's and was last operated on the New Canaan Branch. (Courtesy Bob Lorenz)

THE OPEN END electric MU coaches on the New Haven also included trailer cars. These cars were equipped with full controls and head lights, and therefore could be operated as the lead car of a train. (Courtesy Bob Lorenz)

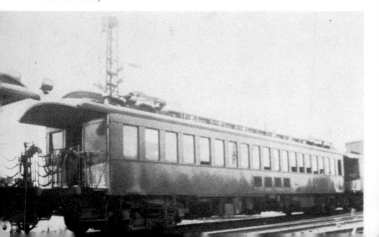

A FAST NEW HAVEN commuter express departing New Haven for Grand Central Terminal behind electric 0302. (Courtesy H. W. Pontin, Rail Photo Service)

STAMFORD, CONNECTICUT is an intermediate terminal in the Penn Central's New York-New Haven suburban district. Most MU trains to or from New York originate or terminate at Stamford and are serviced at the coach yard at that point. (Courtesy Bob Lorenz)

ONE WAY to beat the week-end lay over of suburban equipment is to operate fan trips. Here is such a fan trip on the former New Haven Railroad. The baggage compartment of the combine is used by fans with tape recorders. Note the slats in the open door to prevent accidents. (Courtesy Bob Lorenz)

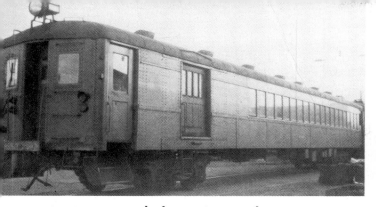 

ON SOME MU suburban train runs, baggage service is offered. When this is the case, equipment such as this baggage combine trailer are operated in the consist of the train. (Courtesy Bob Lorenz)

THE NEW HAVEN REGION, like most other MU operations, also employs trailer coaches in their suburban trains. Here the trailer coach No. 4268 rests between runs at the Stamford, Connecticut yard. (Courtesy Bob Lorenz)

A STANDARD MU suburban train at the Cos Cob Station on the New Haven Division of the New Haven Region. (Courtesy Bob Lorenz)

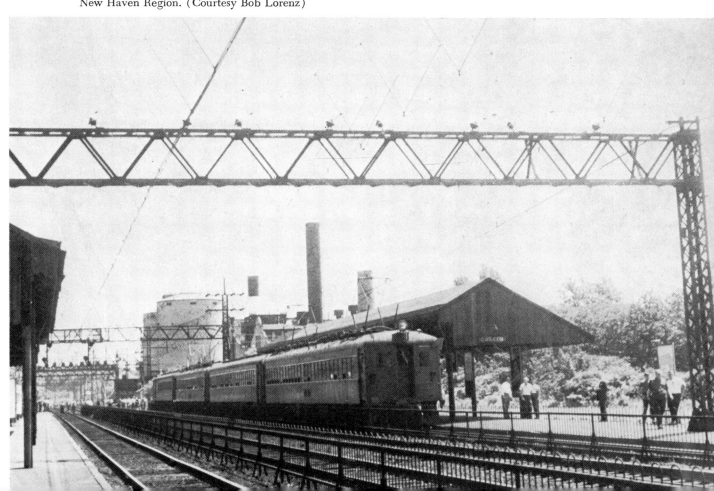

THE NEW HAVEN RAILROAD purchased 100 of these stainless steel suburban coaches from Pullman Standard. These coaches are 85 feet long and a small fleet has been fitted out as Club Cars. This equipment, as with all New Haven Region MU equipment, has a unique electrical design. They are equipped for 11,000 volt pantagraph pick-up, plus 600 volt third rail operation. This means that the New Haven equipment will be able to operate south of New York in the New Jersey or Philadelphia suburban service, or will be able to operate in the former New York Central's Hudson and Harlem suburban territories. (Courtesy Bob Lorenz)

THE EX-NEW HAVEN EMD FL-9's are now providing real merger benefits to the Penn Central. These units, which can operate with their diesel power or utilize third rail for electric power, are now handling through commuter runs on the ex-New York Central Hudson and Harlem Divisions. This eliminates the need for changing power at either Harmon or White Plains. These unique locomotives are now being painted in the Penn Central color scheme. (Courtesy Electro Motive Division)

FORMER NEW HAVEN suburban passenger equipment is now being repainted in the PC green color scheme. All ex-New Haven electric passenger equipment can operate in either the ex-NYC third rail territory or in the ex-PRR overhead wire areas. This will mean an improvement in equipment utilization as the merger benefits are realized. (Courtesy Penn Central)

THE NEW HAVEN REGION of the PC also operates a commuter train between New London and New Haven. For many years, NH train No. 401 carried a through coach New London to New York which was put on the "The Bankers" from Springfield at New Haven. The few commuters from Madison, Guilford, Branford, etc. had a through ride to Grand Central Terminal. Today (1969) however, the New Haven-New London commuter is equipped with an RDC-1 and Grand Central bound suburbanites must change at New Haven. Prior to the RDC operation, the New London-New Haven train was equipped with an RPO-Baggage and an arched roof coach. The equipment is shown here sleeping out the week end at New London. (Courtesy J. Leonard Bachelder)

Chapter 3

NEW YORK

Long Island and New Jersey Service

The Long Island Railroad

The Long Island Railroad is one of the nation's busiest passenger railroads. The average week day passenger load is 260,000 passengers on the 334 mile suburban line. The Railroad is the largest single suburban operation in America and serves nearly all of Long Island.

The Railroad connects New York City with the Long Island suburbs. The hub of the railroad is the suburb of Jamaica, located 11.3 miles east of New York City's Penn Station. Eastward from Jamaica, eight lines spread out to Oyster Bay, Port Jefferson, Greenport (Main Line), Montauk, Hempstead, West Hempstead, Long Beach and Far Rockaway. Westward there are three lines to Penn Station at Manhattan, Flatbush Avenue in Brooklyn and Hunterspoint Avenue in Long Island City. The following table shows the distance of the above terminals from Penn Station.

Terminal	Distance From Penn Station
Port Washington	19.9
Jamaica	11.3
Greenport	96.3
Montauk	117.4
Hempstead	22.0
Oyster Bay	35.0
Port Jefferson	59.4
West Hempstead	22.4
Long Beach	24.6
Far Rockaway	22.8
Hunterspoint Ave.	8.7 (Distance from Jamaica)
Flatbush Ave.	9.3 (Distance from Jamaica)

The Port Washington branch leaves the main line at Woodside, and trains to and from that line do not operate via Jamaica.

Jamaica is one of the world's busiest passenger stations. During the rush hours, trains run through the eight track station on an average of two trains every minute. Jamaica is a transfer station. Trains coming from Manhattan and Brooklyn arrive at Jamaica, and at that point, passengers change trains according to their destination. Nearly all passengers change trains at Jamaica. Inbound passengers change at Jamaica for either Manhattan or Brooklyn.

To handle the large volume of week day traffic, the Long Island operates 665 passenger trains. In addition, there are 135 scheduled equipment trains. These are trains of empties moving to terminals to begin runs or to yards after runs. There are about 425 scheduled trains on Saturdays and Sundays. These trains have been running consistently with over a 93% on time performance.

Train service on the Long Island varies according to section of the Railroad. As stated previously, rush hour traffic is quite busy, busier than any other railroad. On the New York end of the Railroad, off hour traffic varies from 10 to 25 minute headways during the day to the longest gap of 1 hour, 45 minutes after 1:00 A.M. On the eastern end, there are but 4 trains on the Montauk Branch and 2 trains on the Greenport line. Density of system train service is illustrated by the diagram on page 48.

At the present time, new operating plans are beginning to become a reality on the L.I. For example, 620 new electric MU cars are being delivered to the L.I. from the Budd Company. These new streamliners are even carpted in the non-smoking sections and are among the finest suburban equipment ever built. With these new cars, eventually there will be a thru Jamaica type of train operation. The time consuming change will be eliminated, and of course, better and faster service will be provided to the Long Islanders.

As part of the above plan, electrified territory will be expanded to the Western Suffolk County area. When this is completed, 80% of the Long Island's passengers will be traveling on trains that are electric powered from 650 volt-DC third rail. The remaining 20% will travel on Gas Turbine MU trains (Provided present tests are successful.). These MU cars will travel by Turbine on the eastern end of Long Island, and will switch over to third rail in electric territory.

In order to handle the large volume of passengers, the railroad maintains 78 diesel locomotives and 1200 passenger cars. This figure will vary considerably as the new streamlined electric MU's arrive on the property, and the older 60 foot care are retired. In addition, as the electrified territory is expanded and when the new Turbine cars are ordered for the East End, the number of diesels needed will be much less.

The Long Island maintains just about every type of passenger car there is today, except sleeping cars. Besides the familiar owl faced electric MU cars, the road operates baggage cars, standard and streamlined coaches, lounge cars, coaches equipped with bars, parlor cars and open end observation cars. This equipment is not only used in regular suburban service, but also for many types of specials. These include baseball specials, party trains, rail tours, and believe it or not, All-Parlor Car trains.

The All-Parlor car trains run during the late Spring, Summer and early Fall. These trains operate eastbound Thursday and Friday evenings from Long Island City via Jamaica, where they pick up passengers from Penn Station, to Montauk. They return to the New York Area on Sunday evening. These extra fare trains provide luxury travel for people wishing to spend the week-end at the Hamptons, the resort towns on the South Shore of Long Island. These All-Parlor luxury liners are called the "Cannonball" and the "Week-ender."

In addition to the All-Parlor Car trains, the L.I. operates some mixed parlor car-coach trains. These trains operate either on the Montauk Line throughout the week or on week-ends on the Greenport line. These trains operate from Jamaica only.

The railroad was once owned by the Pennsylvania Railroad. However, since January, 1966, the railroad has been wholly owned by the Metropolitan Transportation Authority, but is operated under its own management. The Long Island Area is suffering from severe automobile traffic strangulation. The logical solution is to turn to the Long Island Railroad for efficient transportation instead of building new highways. Now with adequate State support, the Long Island Management is well on their way to reshaping the LI into a show case suburban line that will save time for the suburbanite and save the taxpayer's money—in the form of less highway building and maintenance.

ELECTRIFICATION came to the Long Island Railroad in 1905 when the first section of the 650 volt dc third rail system was installed between Flatbush Avenue and Rockaway Park. At first, steeple cab locomotives did the honors for motive power.

The first electric MU cars, such as the 1007, were placed in service in 1908. In that year, the Hempstead Branch was electrified. The busy Penn Station-Jamaica line was not electrified until 1910. During the next fifteen years the main line to Mineola and south shore line to Babylon was electrified along with the following branch lines: West Hempstead, Long Beach, Far Rockaway, and Port Washington. (Courtesy Bob Lorenz)

DURING THE DAYS OF STEAM, the Long Island owned some of their own steam power, but also leased steam power from their one time parent, the Pennsylvania Railroad. Here four Pennsylvania Railroad K-4's are being serviced between runs at Montauk, Long Island when there were more trains running to Montauk than there is today. (Courtesy Bob Lorenz)

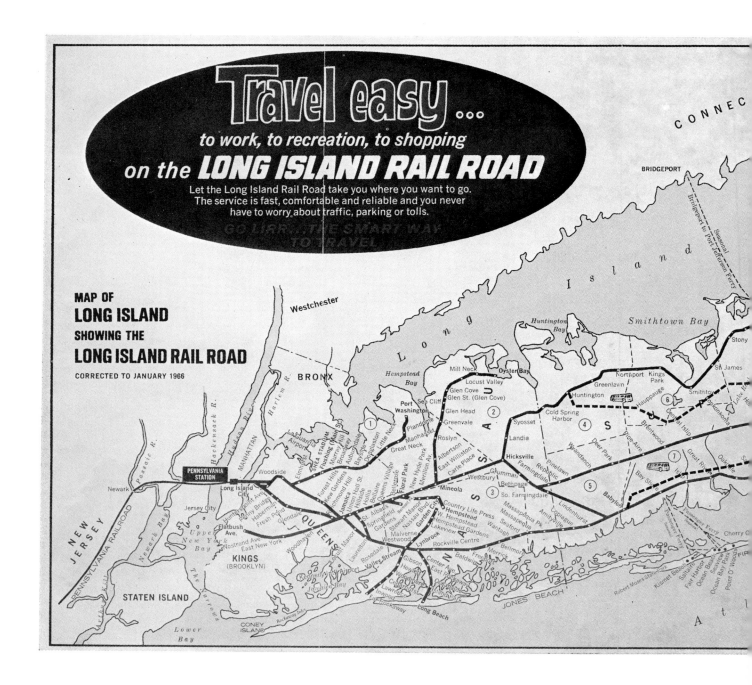

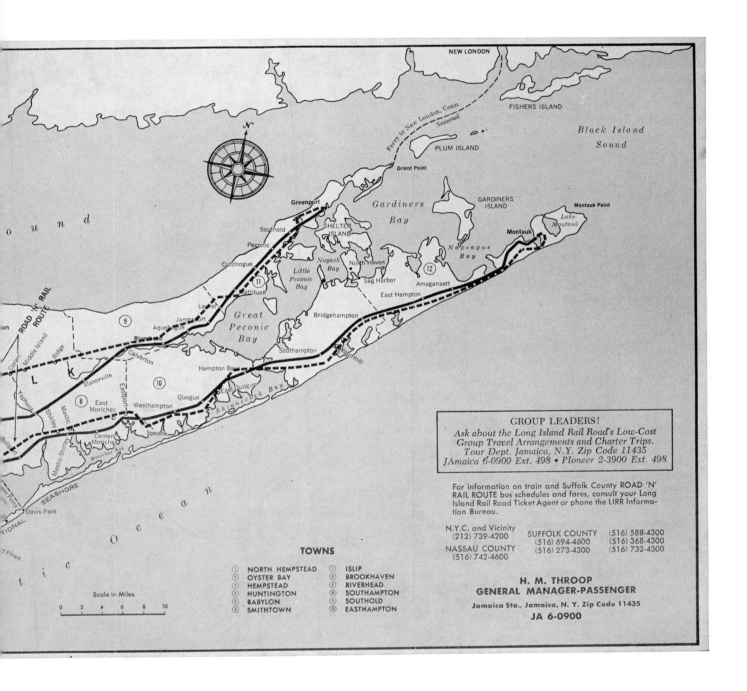

NEW LONDON

FISHERS ISLAND

Block Island Sound

Ferry to New London, Conn.

Seasonal

PLUM ISLAND

Orient Point

Gardiners Bay

GARDINERS ISLAND

Montauk Point

Greenport

Lake Montauk

Southold

SHELTER ISLAND

Peconic

Napeague Bay

Montauk

Cutchogue

Noyack Bay

North Haven

⑫

Mattituck

Little Peconic Bay

Sag Harbor

Amagansett

⑪

Laurel

Jamesport

Great Peconic Bay

East Hampton

Aquebogue

⑨

Bridgehampton

Riverhead

Southampton

Calverton

Watermill

ROAD 'N' RAIL ROUTE

Hampton Bays

Manorville

⑩

Quogue

East Quogue

Shinnecock Bay

L   K

Eastport

⑧ East Moriches

Westhampton

Coram

Middle Island

Ridge

Yaphank

Speonk

Shirley

Mastic

Center Moriches

Moriches Bay

Mastic-Shirley

Bellport

SEASHORE

Davis Park

TIONAL

d Pines

O c e a n

t i c

A t l a n

N

S o u n d

TOWNS

① NORTH HEMPSTEAD
② OYSTER BAY
③ HEMPSTEAD
④ HUNTINGTON
⑤ BABYLON
⑥ SMITHTOWN
⑦ ISLIP
⑧ BROOKHAVEN
⑨ RIVERHEAD
⑩ SOUTHAMPTON
⑪ SOUTHOLD
⑫ EASTHAMPTON

Scale in Miles

0   2   4   6   8   10

FOR MANY YEARS this was the typical passenger train consist in the Long Island's electrified territory. This early rush hour train is on the Far Rockaway line on the south side of Long Island. (Courtesy Bob Lorenz)

A NON RUSH HOUR electric MU Long Island passenger train. (Courtesy Bob Lorenz)

AS YET, much of the equipment on the Long Island is 65 foot, non air conditioned, owl faced electric MU coaches. As time goes on these cars will be replaced by the new Budd Company's "Metropolitans." Seating capacities of these cars ranges from 66 to 98, with most of the coaches being able to seat about 80 passengers. (Courtesy Bob Lorenz)

IN 1968, the Long Island owned and operated 63 double deck suburban coaches. These cars were originally built in the early 1940's and have seating capacities from 120 to 134 passengers, depending upon the style of the car. The Long Island was the first road to use a double deck design in commuter service. However, even though the Chicagoland railroads have invested heavily in double deck coaches with an improved design, the Long Island has thus far elected not to return to such equipment. This train is at the West Hempstead station. Courtesy Bob Lorenz)

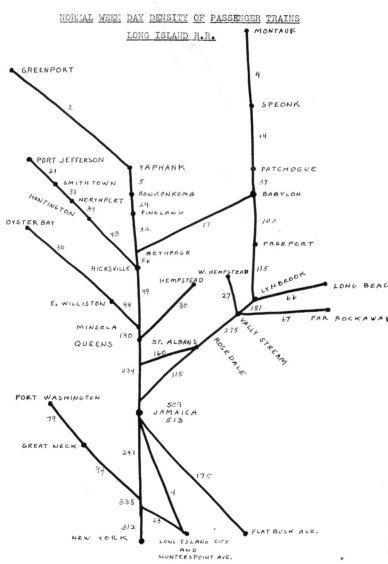

NORMAL WEEK DAY DENSITY OF PASSENGER TRAINS
LONG ISLAND R.R.

THE LONG ISLAND purchased two Rail Diesel Cars in 1955. The two cars were used for various types of assignments until 1967. At that time, the RDC's were involved in a derailment and were taken out of service. The RDC-2 has since been sold to the Baltimore & Ohio Railroad. The RDC-1, is at the time of this writing (1969), stored at Jamaica. (Courtesy Bob Lorenz)

OUTSIDE OF THE electrified territory, The Long Island operates a fleet of Alco Road switchers for passenger train motive power. Here the 1553 is arriving at Roosevelt, Long Island with a conventional train. (Courtesy Bob Lorenz)

THE EXTREME eastern terminal of the Long Island is Montauk. This photo shows the end of the line and the station at that point. When trains arrive at Montauk, they pull right up to the end of the track as shown here. (Courtesy Bob Lorenz)

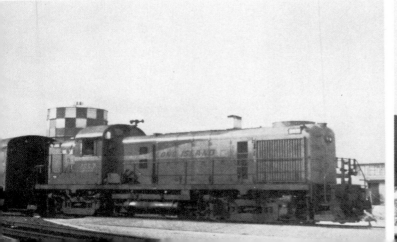

THIRTY COACHES advertising "Your Steel Thru-way to the Fair Gateway" were delivered to the the Long Island in 1963. These cars are similar in design and construction to 53 electric commuter cars delivered to the New York Central in 1962. Of the 30 cars, 12 are cab control units equipped with propulsion equipment, auxiliaries, operating and automatic speed controls. Eighteen are motor trailer coaches with only propulsion equipment and auxiliaries. The air-conditioned and electrically heated cars seat 130 in the cab units and 133 in the trailer cars. (Courtesy Pullman Standard)

THIS PHOTO shows the interior of one of the 30 electric MU passenger cars that the Long Island ordered from Pullman-Standard in 1963. The car interiors were built of decorative materials that require no painting. The body seats are three and two passenger walkover type while bulkhead seats are two passenger lightweight stationary type. Seat cushions and backs are covered with vinyl-plastic-coated fabric and the panel within the arm rest of the seat is unpainted, rigidized stainless steel. (Courtesy Pullman-Standard)

THE LONG ISLAND has recently purchased a number of streamlined coaches from other railroads. This train is made up of ex-New York Central coaches and is known as the "Silver Streak." The motive power is an Alco Century 420. The train has just arrived at Smithtown, Long Island on the Port Jefferson Branch. (Courtesy Bob Lorenz)

THE LONG ISLAND Railroad operates a fleet of Parlor Cars in regular train service. This particular car is the 2024, the "Copiague" and was formerly owned by the Pennsylvania Railroad. The car was built by Pullman Standard and is 82 feet 11 inches long. The seating capacity is 33 passengers. This scene is at Montauk Yard in 1967. (Courtesy Bob Lorenz)

THE NEW "METROPOLITAN" suburban passenger cars, now in operation on the Long Island, are arranged in two car units completely equipped for independent operation. One car in each unit contains batteries and a motor alternator, while the other houses the air compressor. The new coaches have electrically operated double doors located at points approximately one quarter the distance from each end of the car. The doors were designed for high level platforms, which have been built throughout the electrified zone. The new equipment will replace approximately 500 old standard MU coaches. (Courtesy Long Island Railroad)

THE NEW METROPOLITAN coaches feature a three and two seating arrangement. The seats are contoured and upholstered in a durable, washable fabric over a foam base of at least four inches thick. The floors are covered with rubber tile and carpeting, and the cars are soundproofed to eliminate outside noise. The cars are equipped with modern aircraft type lavatories with hot and cold running water and electric hand dryers. There is a crew to passenger public address system. The "Metropolitan" has a cruising speed of 100 MPH. (Courtesy Long Island Railroad)

WHEN THE NEW "METROPOLITANS" went into service, the Press and TV rode a number of trains to photograph, film and tape the commuter's reaction to the new trains. This photo shows a rush hour train with a TV crew filming the crowded car. (Courtesy Long Island Railroad)

AS WITH ALL NEW passenger equipment, the Long Island placed the Metropolitans on display before they went into actual service. In this case, two of the new cars are on display at Jamaica. This photo shows very clearly a new style automatic coupler, the dual head lights, the low level red marker lights and the streamlined nose for less wind resistence. (Courtesy The Budd Company)

THE LONG ISLAND is not only purchasing new electric equipment, but is also testing with the Budd Company, self contained turbine cars. If successful, the Long Island will acquire a fleet of turbine coaches which will draw electric power from Third Rail in electrified territory, and will operate under turbine power in non-electrified areas. (Courtesy The Budd Company)

The Penn Central Company

The Penn Central serves the Northern New Jersey suburbs between New York City and Trenton, New Jersey, a distance of 58.1 miles. The Penn Central also operates trains over the subsidiary New York & Long Branch Railroad to Bay Head Junction. Bay Head Junction is 66.6 miles from New York City. The entire Main Line service is electrified with overhead wire, while the NY&LB is electrified only as far as South Amboy.

The Trenton Line and the Long Branch trains carry an average of 42,500 weekday passengers. To handle this volume, the PC operates 63 weekday suburban trains in each direction. Most of these trains originate or terminate at New Brunswick. Nineteen of the above trains operate in each direction to and from the Long Branch Line. Additional service is provided by certain through trains that stop at Newark, Elizabeth and Trenton. This section of railroad is one of the busiest in the Nation.

As usual, during the rush hours, this line is even busier then it is during the rest of the day. On week days, from 6:30 A.M. to 9:00 A.M., there are 18 suburban train arrivals at New York's Penn Station. This number does not include those thru trains that make certain stops within the suburban territory. There are 19 suburban train departures from Penn Station to New Jersey points from 4:00 P.M. to 7:00 P.M.

Train service on the Trenton Line begins shortly after 5:00 A.M. and continues until after 1:00 A.M. Non rush hour traffic between New York and New Brunswick varies from 10 to 50 minute intervals, with most of the service 20 to 25 minutes apart. The frequency of service depends upon the time of day. Saturday service sees 22 westbound and 23 eastbound suburban trains. Sunday service consists of 14 westbound and 16 eastbound trains.

Train service on the Main Line is handled by 35 streamlined electric MU coaches. These cars are unique in that they have both center doors and end vestibule doors for loading and unloading at both high level and ground level station platforms respectively. At the present time, the PC is also using a number of standard MU cars in this territory. These will soon be replaced by an additional 45 streamlined cars identical to the above 35. This Multiple Unit equipment is also used to provide train service on the New York & Long Branch Railroad only as far south as South Amboy. Nine of the nineteen trains in each direction on the NY&LB originate and terminate at South Amboy, the present limits of the electrified territory.

The State of New Jersey has authorized a capital improvement program for the NY&LB. This includes the order of 38 electric MU coaches, complete electrification, new stations with high level platforms and elimination of grade crossings. At the present time, the PC is operating 10 trains in each direction between New York City and Bay Head Junction. This reduces to 6 and 4 on Saturday and Sunday respectively.

The Penn Central also operates Refreshment Car service on the morning and evening rush hour trains on the NY&LB. Through New York City and Bay Head Junction trains are diesel powered with road switchers, and are equipped with standard coaches.

Growing acceptance of public assistance in New Jersey has enabled the PC to cut its operating deficit for this service, and has expedited the acquisition of new equipment. This means that the PC has been able to improve its service to the public, and hopefully less highways and parking ramps will now have to be built; which means a tax dollar savings for the public.

THE PENN CENTRAL COMPANY
NEW JERSEY SUBURBAN TERRITORY

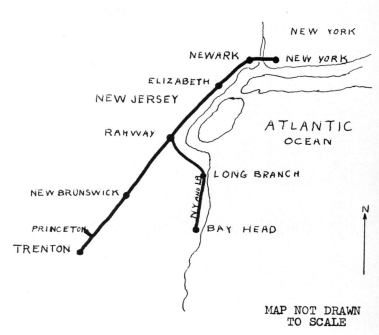

MAP NOT DRAWN TO SCALE

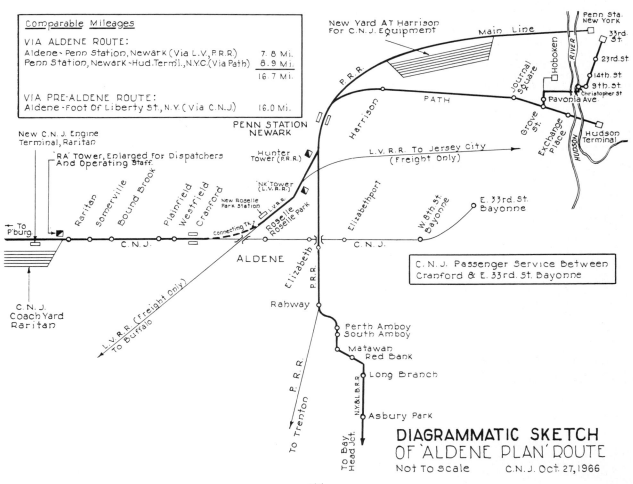

Comparable Mileages

VIA ALDENE ROUTE:
Aldene - Penn Station, Newark (Via L.V., P.R.R.) 7.8 Mi.
Penn Station, Newark - Hud.Terml., N.Y.C. (Via Path) 8.9 Mi.
                                                      16.7 Mi.

VIA PRE-ALDENE ROUTE:
Aldene - Foot Of Liberty St., N.Y. (Via C.N.J.) 16.0 Mi.

C.N.J. Passenger Service Between Cranford & E. 33rd. St. Bayonne

DIAGRAMMATIC SKETCH OF 'ALDENE PLAN' ROUTE
Not To Scale   C.N.J. Oct. 27, 1966

55

THE PENNSYLVANIA RAILROAD operated Pacific type steam locomotives over the non electrified portion of the New York and Long Branch Railroad. Here two K-4's head up two rush hour commuter trains. The last car on the first commuter train is a Dining—Refreshment car. Such equipment is still being operated on the Penn Central Long Branch trains in 1969. (Courtesy Bob Lorenz)

ON THE PENN CENTRAL, or ex-Pennsy suburban service on the New York & Long Branch, conventional power must be exchanged for electric power at South Amboy for the run through the tunnels to the Penn Station at New York. This photo of changing power was taken after a K4 was released from its duty and a GG 1 was preparing to speed the NY&LB suburban passenger train to New York City. Power exchanges will be eliminated completely when the NY&LB is electrified through to Bay Head Junction. (Courtesy G. C. Corey, Rail Photo Service)

IN ADDITION to the new streamlined suburban coaches, the Penn Central operates a large fleet of these 65 foot electric multiple unit coaches in their North New Jersey commuter service. These coaches have a seating capacity of 72 passengers and a cruising speed of 65 Miles Per Hour. The cars are operated with electric trailer coaches of the same length and seating capacity. (Courtesy Bob Lorenz)

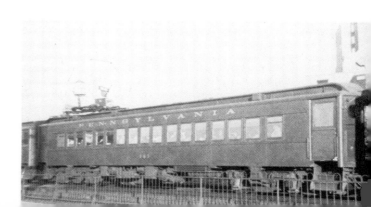

A NEW YORK and Long Branch Pennsy suburban train southbound for Bay Head Junction after leaving the electrified territory at South Amboy. K4's did the honors during the days of steam—now road switchers and excess E units perform the same task with the same steel equipment used in the days of steam. (Courtesy G. C. Corey, Rail Photo Service)

A PENN CENTRAL electric suburban train arriving at Elizabeth, New Jersey on the Main Line of the New Jersey Division. (Courtesy Bob Lorenz)

AT THE PRESENT TIME, the New York and Long Branch is electrified as far as South Amboy, New Jersey. At that point, the PC maintains a small electric coach yard for the overnight storage of suburban equipment. Trains beyond South Amboy are diesel powered. (Courtesy Bob Lorenz)

THE PENN CENTRAL operates a suburban connecting service on the Princeton, N. J. Branch Line. The branch extends from Princeton Junction to Princeton, a distance of 2.7 miles. Princeton Junction is 48.4 miles from Pennsylvania Station in New York City. Service on the branch is scheduled for connection with Main Line New York City—Trenton suburban trains. Main line crews are instructed to wait five minutes at Princeton Junction for the Princeton trains. Running time on the branch is 4 to 5 minutes including a stop at Penns Neck. All trains on the Princeton Branch are handled by MU electric coaches. This photo shows the shuttle train at the end of the line at Princeton. (Courtesy Bob Lorenz)

THIS STREAMLINED SUBURBAN COACH is the newest style to be operated on the American Railroads. This car and 34 others are currently in operation on the Penn Central between New York City's Penn Station and Trenton, New Brunswick and South Amboy. These cars have a cruising speed of 100 mph and have a high comfort index. In addition, the cars are equipped with both high-level center doors as well as combination high/low side doors located near the end. This arrangement permits passengers to enter and leave with much greater ease than was possible with the older MU cars operated by the Penn Central. (Courtesy General Steel Industries)

THE INTERIORS of the new General Steel Industries suburban coaches feature beige-and-blue color schemes throughout accentuated with wood grain finish highlights. Each car has 118 contoured high-back seats that are arranged with three seats on one side and two on the other. The cars are divided into two sections separated by a center vestibule. In one section smoking is permitted. (Courtesy Penn Central Co.)

THE PENN CENTRAL has a number of commuters that travel from Philadelphia to New York City and return each working day. These passengers ride the through streamliners and metroliners between those two points. This photo shows a new metroliner in a test run prior to going into regular service. (Courtesy The Budd Company)

Erie Lackawanna Railroad

The Erie Lackawanna operates a major suburban service to the New York suburbs in New Jersey. There are four suburban lines plus three branches. These lines radiate from north to west from Hoboken Terminal across the river from New York City. The north line; from Hoboken to Spring Valley, a distance of 30.6 miles; was formerly the New Jersey and New York Railroad. It is now known as the NJ& NY Branch. The next line, to the northwest, is known as the New York Division Main Line and the Bergen County Line. In this case, most of the suburban service extends to Suffern, 30.5 miles from Hoboken, but there is additional service to Port Jervis, 87.2 miles from Hoboken. The next line is known as the Greenwood Lake-Boonton Line. This line goes through Dover to Netcong, 48.4 miles from Hoboken. The last line extends west to Dover, which is 40.5 miles from Hoboken. There are two branches on this route, known as the Montclair Branch and the Gladstone Branch. Montclair and Gladstone are located 13.1 and 42.3 miles respectively from Hoboken.

The Erie Lackawanna carries nearly 65,000 week day passengers on these various routes. In order to provide service for the suburbanite, the EL operates a total of 241 week day trains. This number reduces to 56 and 35 on Saturday and Sunday respectively. All EL trains operate into Hoboken Terminal. At this point, passengers transfer to or from Port Authority Trans Hudson (PATH) rapid transit trains for New York City service, or to buses operated by the Public Service Coordinated Transport. Bus service operates to and from 41st St. & 8th Ave. in Manhattan. PATH service to and from Hoboken Terminal varies from every three minutes to 20 min-

utes according to passenger volume and the time of day. During the morning rush hours, there are 46 arrivals at Hoboken. The evening rush has 44 departures. Rush hour service makes up about 33% of EL's total suburban schedules.

The individual line operations are quite interesting. The New Jersey and New York line is the simplest. Here there are only 5 Rush Hour trains in each direction between Hoboken and Spring Valley. There is no Saturday or Sunday service. Standard coaches pulled by 1500-1600 HP EMD and Alco road switchers are used on this line.

The service to Suffern and Port Jervis is actually operated over two lines, known as the Main Line and the Bergen County Line. The latter leaves the Main Line near Rutherford and rejoins it near Glen Rock. Trains operate over both lines in both directions. There are 54 week day trains on this line. Most of the inbound trains originate at Waldwick (Waldwick is located 7.3 miles east of Suffern.) and Suffern, but one originates from Monroe and two from Port Jervis. Most of the outbound trains terminate at Walkwick and Suffern with three terminating at Ridgewood and two at Port Jervis. Equipment used on this line is standard coaches pulled by 1500 and 1600 HP Alco and EMD road switchers and EMD 2250 HP E-8's.

Off hour service on the Suffern line varies from 90 to 120 minutes. Service begins after 5 A.M. and continues until 11:30 P.M. Saturday service sees four trains in each direction, with no service on Sunday.

The Dover and Netcong service on the Greenwood Lake Boonton line consists of 8 Rush Hour trains in each direction only. All trains originate or terminate at Dover, except one train to and from Netcong. Equipment used on this line is the same as used on the Suffern-Port Jervis service. There is no

Saturday or Sunday service on this line.

To provide train service on the three above lines, the EL maintains 179 standard coaches.

The Morristown Line, including the Montclair and Gladstone branches, is the electrified portion of EL's suburban service. This line is the busiest also with 134 week day trains. This reduces to 48 and 35 on Saturdays and Sundays. Most trains originate or terminate at Dover, however a few operate only to and from Morristown. Week day service ranges from 5:00 A.M. until after mid-night.

The Gladstone branch is served either by thru rush hour trains, or by thru cars that are carried on trains to or from Dover. Westbound, these cars are detached at Summit and then run on their own to Gladstone. Eastbound, the reverse is true. There are 14 week day trains in each direction on this branch. On Saturday, there are 7 trains in each direction with Sunday service reduced to 5 each way. The operating procedures for the thru cars to and from the Gladstone branch are quite simple because of the electric MU train operation.

Service on the Montclair branch consists of 12 weekday trains in each direction between Hoboken and Montclair. There is no Saturday or Sunday service on this branch line.

Motive power and cars are serviced and cleaned during lay over time at Hoboken. Equipment is stored overnight with some servicing at the following points: Dover, Netcong, Spring Valley, Gladstone, Suffern, Waldwick and Port Jervis.

At the present time, the EL is grossing approximately $9 million annually. They have an annual operating deficit calculated on an avoidable cost basis of nearly $5 million. This loss is reimbursed to the EL through contract payments by the State of New Jersey.

The State of New Jersey has been working on a plan for improving and/or expanding the entire suburban service operated in that State. This involves not only financial assistance plans, but also the purchase of new equipment for leasing to the suburban railroads. The Erie Lackawanna is involved in this plan. New electric MU cars, similar to those now in operation in the New York-Trenton service on the Penn Central, are planned for the EL's service.

The population density of New Jersey is now greater than that of India's. Highway traffic is choking the transportation flow. The State has realized the fact that it is quite difficult for private investors to earn a satisfactory return on their investment in rail suburban service. The highway expansion program is in the state of diminishing returns. Because of the above conditions, the Erie Lackawanna Suburban Service can now look forward to a much brighter future.

THERE WAS NO ELECTRIFICATION on the former Erie Railroad. Therefore, prior to dieselization, steam power did the honors for the commuter service. During the early 1940's, the Erie operated a delux commuter train between Hoboken and Port Jervis, "The Tuxedo." The train carried parlor cars in addition to the usual commuter coaches. The Erie was one of very few railroads to operate parlor cars in regular commuter assignments. Today, the "Tuxedo" has lost its parlor cars and its name is no longer listed in the timetables. However the train is now powered by a sleek EMD 2250 HP E-8 diesel passenger unit and it still provides the same fast convenient service to and from Port Jervis as was provided in the early 1940's. (Courtesy Bob Lorenz)

AN EVENING RUSH HOUR line up of Erie commuter trains in the former Erie Terminal. Ten suburban trains can be seen awaiting the high ball to various suburban terminals. The New York City sky line is visible in the right hand side of the photo. (Courtesy Jack Dimond)

THE ERIE LACKAWANNA operates several Electro Motive Division diesel units in its suburban service. GP-9's and E-8's are assigned to all commuter runs except the electrified service. All units, both ex Erie units and ex DL&W units are painted in the former Lackawanna color scheme with the new EL herald. (Courtesy Jack Dimond)

AN ERIE LACKAWANNA rush hour suburban train powered by Alco Road Switcher 926 (1500 HP unit equipped with steam generator) with a consist of a combination coach, and five Stillwell coaches. These cars will be replaced as soon as modernization plans can be carried out by the State of New Jersey. (Courtesy Jack Dimond)

THE ERIE LACKAWANNA RAILROAD

NEW JERSEY SUBURBAN TERRITORY

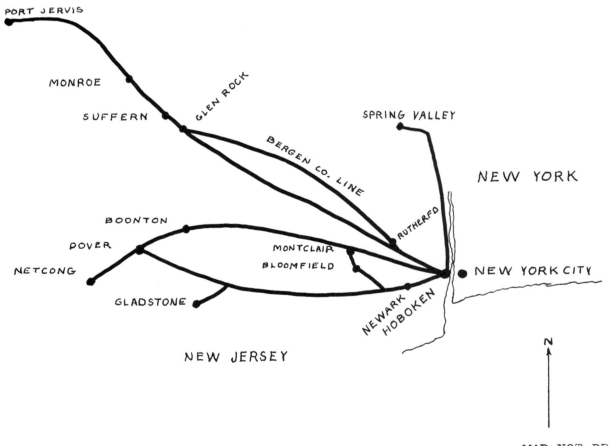

DURING THE 1920'S, the Delaware, Lackawanna & Western's Hoboken Terminal was highly congested with steam locomotives, both switchers and road engines, and commuter and long distance passenger trains. This congestion, which resulted in many delays, brought about the decision in 1928 to electrify the suburban railroad service. The decision was also made to use electric MU equipment because of its rapid acceleration, more flexible off peak hour operations and the enormous reduction in switching moves for suburban train assembly.

The company's 3000 volt dc overhead catenary system was completed in 1931, and since that time there has been very little change in the original catenary installation. (Courtesy Bob Lorenz)

BETWEEN RUNS, Erie Lackawanna stores and services MU equipment at the Dover coach yard. This view shows 20 electric MU coaches awaiting assignments to Hoboken Terminal. The EL also stores and services MU equipment at Gladstone. (Courtesy Bob Lorenz)

Central Railroad of New Jersey

The Central Railroad Company of New Jersey operates a suburban railroad passenger service over three lines in the Newark Area. The Company handles or carries 12,000 weekday passengers in each direction, and grosses nearly $4 million yearly on their service. However, the annual deficit on this service is approximately $7 million. In order to preserve this passenger service, and to lower the costs of building and maintaining super highways, the State of New Jersey by contractual arrangement, is supplying the CNJ with sufficient funds in order to absorb a substantial portion of this loss.

The CNJ suburban train operations are quite complicated when compared to most operations of this type. Not only does the CNJ operate on its own trackage, but also over the Penn Central and the Lehigh Valley. Their trains also operate over a subsidiary railroad, the New York and Long Branch Railroad.

The Railroad provides commuter service between Newark and Hampton, a distance of 49.9 miles; a shuttle service between Bayonne and Cranford, a distance of 11.2 miles; and between Newark and Bay Head Junction, a distance of 56.6 miles. The latter service is partially over the New York and Long Branch, which owns no equipment of its own. The NY&LB extends for 39 miles between Perth Amboy and Bay Head Junction. The Penn Central also runs commuter trains over the NY&LB RR. Passengers from CNJ points en route to or from New York transfer at Newark to either Penn Central

trains or to Port Authority Trans-Hudson (PATH) rail rapid transit system.

The CNJ operates a total of 106 passenger trains over the three routes. There are 50 operated on the Main Line to Raritan with 4 operated beyond to Hampton, 42 in shuttle service between the Main Line at Cranford to Bayonne and 14 on the New York and Long Branch. The train service frequency breaks down as follows: On the Main Line, there are 23 trains in each direction between Raritan and Newark. There are two additional trains in each direction between Newark and Hampton. During the rush hours from 6 to 9 A.M. and 4 to 6 P.M., there are 10 arrivals and 7 departures respectively at Newark. The other trains are operated on frequencies of 60 to 75 minutes until shortly after midnight. The Cranford-Bayonne shuttle trains meet all Main Line trains at Cranford. Main Line Saturday service reduces to 18 trains with a Sunday service of 13 trains in each direction. The week end shuttle service matches the Main Line Schedules.

The CNJ operates 7 weekday trains in each direction over the NY&LB. Five of these are operated to and from Newark during the morning and evening rush hours respectively. The other two trains operate in the afternoon and evening. Saturday and Sunday service consists of 5 and 3 trains in each direction respectively. The Penn Central operates 19 weekday trains in each direction on the New York and Long Branch, and therefore, provides the bulk of the non rush hour service.

The Aldene Plan provides that CNJ trains operate into Newark instead of Jersey City. Trains from the

A **WESTBOUND** "All Steel" commuter evening rush hour train arriving Plainfield, New Jersey behind Tank Engine No. 223 just before the stock market crash in 1929. (Courtesy H. W. Pontin, Rail Photo Service)

NY&LB operate over the Penn Central from a point just north of Perth Amboy (See diagrammatic sketch of Aldene Plan Route.) to Penn Station at Newark. Trains from the Main Line operate on the CNJ to Aldene Junction. From that point they operate over the Lehigh Valley Railroad to NK Tower. From there they operate over the PC to Newark.

In order to furnish train service for New Jersey commuters, the CNJ maintains and operates 65 rebuilt standard coaches, of which 38 are equipped for push pull service on the Main Line; 50 streamlined coaches and 11 Rail Diesel Cars. Motive power is provided by 13 GP-40's. These locomotives handle all CNJ passenger trains, except for the RDC service. Train lengths vary from two car scoots to 10, 12 and 13 car trains during the rush hours. During the day, the cars and locomotives are serviced at Harrison Yard, just east of the Newark Station. The trains are stored overnight at Raritan on the Main Line, and at Bay Head Junction on the New York & Long Branch. The shuttle trains are also stored at Raritan. The first train to be dispatched from Raritan in the early morning is the equipment for the shuttle service.

The above service is quite a change from the old style of service. For example, passengers enroute to New York have a choice of mid town or down town Manhattan destinations by PC or PATH rail service, instead of to the downtown area only by the former ferry boat service from Jersey City. The CNJ could not by itself finance such an undertaking as the Aldene Plan. The State of New Jersey has appropriated several million dollars and has obtained a Federal Grant under the Urban Mass Transportation Act of 1964. With these funds and the co-operation of the State of New Jersey, the CNJ is now able to continue passenger service. However, much work needs to be done before the Railroad is out of the Financial Woods.

Future plans are divided into two more phases. The State has indicated it plans to improve stations along the CNJ main line from Cranford to Raritan with high level platforms and enlarged parking lots. The last phase includes State plans for the electrification of major portions of the CNJ and the NY&LB Railroads. The electric MU cars that are to be purchased, will be quite similar to the newest center vestibule cars that are now in service on the Penn Central's New York-Trenton line. With these changes and improvements will come more frequent service; and hopefully will help put the CNJ back on a solid financial footing.

DURING THE DAYS OF STEAM, the Central Railroad of New Jersey used a number of Camel Backs in suburban service. Here the engineer is awaiting the high ball after loading passengers at Freehold, New Jersey on a two car non rush hour train. (Courtesy Bob Lorenz)

AT THE PRESENT TIME, the CNJ owns 11 RDC-1's. Four of these cars, numbers 558 through 561 were originally owned by the New York, Susquehanna & Western Railroad, a company that no longer operates suburban passenger service. The cars are operated between all points in the CNJ's suburban territory. (Courtesy CNJ)

AN EASTBOUND CNJ RDC train passing Westfield, New Jersey. Note the standard coach behind the first RDC. This practice is no longer followed on the CNJ. (Courtesy CNJ)

A PORTRAIT of former Central Railroad of New Jersey suburban equipment before the State began its modernization program. The standard coaches have been repainted inside and out, and many equipped for push pull operation. The RDC's have been freshened up and no longer operate with standard coaches in their consist. The GP-9's have been replaced with brand new elongated GP-40's and in general the image is much improved. This photo typifies either the intermediate or the far out suburban train storage area, where very few trains are stored or serviced. The photo was taken on a quiet week-end afternoon at Highland, New Jersey. (Courtesy Bob Lorenz)

PRIOR TO THE PURCHASE of the elongated GP-40's, the CNJ powered suburban trains with Fairbanks-Morse 2400 HP Trainmaster Type diesel electrics. In this scene, the 2406 is heading up a 14 car rush hour limited at Jersey City, New Jersey. Trains, such as this one, are no longer operating to Jersey City since the Aldene Plan went into effect. (Courtesy Bob Lorenz)

THE CNJ MAINTAINS and operates 65 standard coaches in suburban service. Of these 38 are equipped for such pull operation. This photo shows a standard coach, which has been rebuilt and equipped with a cab. All of the standard coaches now in use have received all necessary body repairs, painting and complete overhaul of trucks and running gear and complete refurbishing of the interiors. The exterior color of this equipment is dark blue and CNJ's 'Miss Liberty' insignia and the car number appear in gold on each side. (Courtesy CNJ)

THE STATEN ISLAND Rapid Transit began life in the late 19th Century as an Interurban on Staten Island. Today, the Company is controlled by the B&O and might be more appropriately called an "Intraurban" as the entire service is on Staten Island, the Richmond Borough, the city of New York. The company uses third rail rapid transit equipment between St. George and Tottenville. Service between Manhattan and Staten Island is provided by Municipal Ferry. Train service ranges from 15 minute frequencies during the day to hourly from mid-night to 5 AM. (Courtesy Bob Lorenz)

THIS CENTRAL RAILROAD Company of New Jersey suburban train is on the New York & Long Branch Railroad. The locomotive is one of the new GP-40's that are equipped with steam generators. The passenger cars are among those recently purchased from the Rock Island. These cars are of stainless steel construction, air conditioned and feature reclining, turn-around seats as well as both over seat and over aisle lighting. Interior color combinations vary from car to car, but all colors are complementary and attractive. One example of the interior color schemes is cream and tan with light green seat upholstery. (Courtesy CNJ)

Chapter 4
PHILADELPHIA

The Reading Company

The Reading Company operates a suburban territory over seven lines that spread eagle from northeast to northwest of Philadelphia. The company grosses approximately $6.8 million annually on their suburban operation. Most of the service is now under an Assistance Program through the Southeastern Pennsylvania Transportation Authority. It costs the Railroad approximately $12.5 million for providing this service, which means a $5.0 million deficit. They are reimbursed $4.9 million in contract payments by SEPTA. This means that the Reading has an annual deficit of about $100,000. This is approximately the amount of the loss for service not covered by the SEPTA contract.

At the present time, the Reading is carrying an average of 43,800 week day passengers. To handle this volume, the Company operates 376 week day trains. This number reduces to 257 on Saturday and 108 on Sunday. Most of these trains operate to Philadelphia, however not all of them operate into the Reading Terminal.

Rush hour traffic on most of the Reading Suburban lines is heavier then off hour traffic, but it only represents about 22% of the total trains operated. On some railroads, the rush hour traffic constitutes 50% or more of their service—but not so on the Reading. From 6:00 A.M. until 9:00 A.M., there are 61 arrivals at Reading Terminal. In the evening, from 4:00 P.M. until 6:30 P.M., there are 67 departures to the suburbs.

A NON RUSH HOUR suburban train enroute to Philadelphia at Landsdale, Pennsylvania on the Doylestown line of the Reading Railroad System. (Courtesy Bob Lorenz)

Off hour service is excellent. The following table shows the mileage from Reading Terminal and Off Hour Train Frequency to the various suburban terminals.

Suburban Terminal	Distance From Reading Terminal	Average Week Day Off Hour Train Frequency
Norristown	18.0	30 to 60 minutes
Hatboro	18.6	30 to 60 minutes
Chestnut Hill	10.8	30 minutes
West Trenton	32.5	60 minutes
New Town	26.3	120 to 240 minutes
Doylestown	34.4	60 to 120 minutes
Lansdale	24.4	30 minutes
Fox Chase	11.0	30 to 180 minutes
Quakertown	40.2	120 to 240 minutes
Glenside-Jenkintown	11.9	15 to 30 minutes

Service begins after 5:00 A.M. and generally runs until mid-night on all lines. Saturday and Sunday frequency is about two thirds and one third of the week day service respectively.

In order to provide such frequent service, the Reading maintains quite a stable of passenger equipment. All lines except the Newtown and the Quakertown lines are electrified. These two exceptions are handled by 16 Rail Diesel Cars. On the other lines, the company uses 108 electric multiple unit standard coaches with 28 trailer coaches, and 17 Silverliners. The Standard MU cars have been going through a rehabilitation program.

It is interesting to note that Reading passenger service is coordinated with local transit service. Besides connecting schedules, combination SEPTA Bus-Reading Rail tickets may be purchased. This cooperation benefits not only the transportation corporations, but the public as well.

The Reading operation is running today through the co-operation of an assistance program thru SEPTA. Without it, the Reading could not continue to provide the fast, modern service that is in operation today. It is an example of sound thinking on the part of local Government, which means possibly fewer highways and parking ramps will be built because of it. Hopefully this type of thinking will spread to other areas of the Nation.

READING COMPANY electric MU train passing the Wayne Junction electric car yards at Philadelphia. (Courtesy Bob Lorenz)

TWO READING SILVERLINERS between runs at the Norristown Coach Yard. (Courtesy Bob Lorenz)

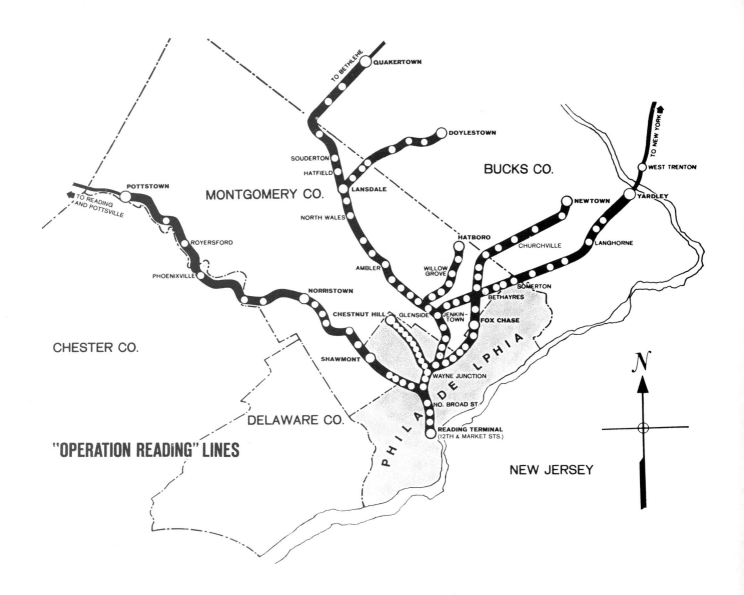

QUAKERTOWN
TO BETHLEHE

DOYLESTOWN

BUCKS CO.

SOUDERTON

HATFIELD

LANSDALE

MONTGOMERY CO.

WEST TRENTON

TO NEW YORK

NEWTOWN

YARDLEY

NORTH WALES

HATBORO

CHURCHVILLE

LANGHORNE

POTTSTOWN

TO READING
AND POTTSVILLE

ROYERSFORD

AMBLER

WILLOW
GROVE

SOMERTON

PHOENIXVILLE

NORRISTOWN

BETHAYRES

CHESTNUT HILL

GLENSIDE

JENKIN-
TOWN

FOX CHASE

CHESTER CO.

SHAWMONT

WAYNE JUNCTION

NO. BROAD ST.

P H I L A D E L P H I A

DELAWARE CO.

"OPERATION READING" LINES

READING TERMINAL
(12TH & MARKET STS.)

NEW JERSEY

N

THE WAYNE JUNCTION Electric Car Shop. (Courtesy The Reading Company)

THE WAYNE JUNCTION Electric Car Yard is located 5.1 miles from the Reading Terminal in Philadelphia. (Courtesy The Reading Company)

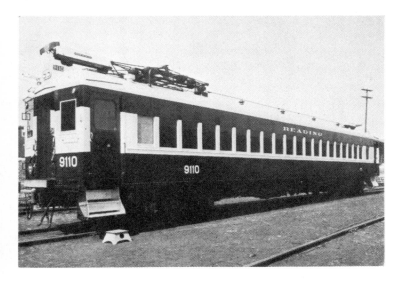

THE READING COMPANY has been rebuilding its 1930 vintage electric MU cars. This particular coach has a seating capacity of 86 passengers and is 73 feet long. (Courtesy Reading Company)

THE READING COMPANY operates 16 Rail Diesel Cars. Except for one RDC-2 and one RDC-3, all of the cars are RDC-1's. The Reading was the last company to acquire new RDC's, and this type of equipment handles all suburban service outside of the electrified territory. (Courtesy Reading Company)

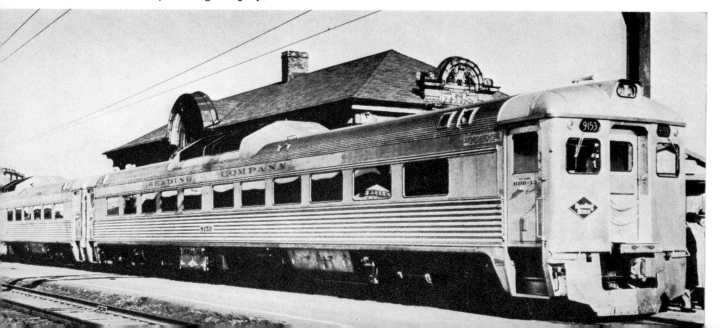

PHILADELPHIA—NEW YORK CITY commuters have a choice of two routes between the two large cities, the Reading—Central Railroad of New Jersey or the Penn Central. Although the Penn Central is the big gun on the route, the Reading and CNJ have teamed up to offer a fast convenient service along their route. Two trains are operated to New York in the morning, and to Philadelphia in the evening. The trains are known as the "Wall Street" and the "Crusader," and they are operated approximately 60 minutes apart in each direction. The accomodations include reclining seat coaches and a Refreshment Car. These cars serve coffee, juice and pastry on the morning trips and beverages on the evening trips. This photo shows the original "Crusader" equipment which consisted of four coaches and a diner-lounge. This equipment has since been sold to the Canadian National Railway. (Courtesy The Budd Company)

STANDARD ELECTRIC MU coaches are still in wide use in the Philadelphia area. Except for the overhead wire power arrangement, the standard coaches are quite similar to the Long Island 65 foot MU suburban equipment. As the reader will remember, the Long Island's power pick up is through third rail. The similarities between the two Railroads' equipment is natural since the Pennsylvania Railroad once owned the Long Island. (Courtesy Penn Central Company)

The Penn Central Company

The Penn Central serves a vast suburban territory northeast, north, west and south of the City of Philadelphia. In fact, this operation is the second largest suburban train operation for the PC; the largest being the New York City service. The PC operates over 3 main lines and 3 branch lines from Philadelphia that spread eagle Southeastern Pennsylvania and extend into New Jersey and Delaware.

The following table shows the distance of suburban terminals from Philadelphia's Penn Center Suburban Station.

Suburban Terminal	Mileage
Bryn Mawr	10.3
Paoli	19.8
Harrisburg	104.6
Chestnut Hill	11.9
Wilmington, Dela.	26.6
Media	14.0
West Chester	27.4
Trenton, N. J.	33.2
Manayunk	7.8

operate to or from Penn Center but do stop at 30th Street or North Philadelphia. Passengers destined mid-city Philadelphia can transfer to suburban trains at either of those two points. Week end suburban service consists of a total of 244 Saturday trains and 113 trains on Sundays and Holidays.

Rush hour service makes up about 27% of the total suburban service. Between 6:00 A.M. and 9:00 A.M., there are 57 arrivals at the Philadelphia Penn Center Suburban Terminal. The evening rush from 4:00 P.M. to 6:30 P.M. sees 56 departures from Philadelphia to the various suburbs.

The following table gives a complete break down of suburban service in the Philadelphia area by individual line.

The trains listed above do not include the through trains operated on the main lines. Through trains play an important part in the total suburban picture in the Philadelphia area. Passengers northeast to or from Trenton have approximately half hourly service with the Washington-Philadelphia-New York-Boston trains. South of Philadelphia, passengers to or from Wilmington have approximately hourly service on the same trains. On the line to

Suburban Terminal To or From Philadelphia	Week Days				Week Ends			
	Total		Rush Hour 6-9AM 4-6:30PM		Sat.		Sun. & Hol.	
	In	Out	In	Out	In	Out	In	Out
Chestnut Hill	38	37	9	9	26	26	10	10
Media	38	38	11	10	27	27	12	11
West Chester	10	9	(1)	(1)	3	3	0	0
Bryn Mawr	63	64	18	19	(3)	(3)	(3)	(3)
Paoli	44	45	(2)	(2)	32	32	21	22
Harrisburg	8	8	(2)	(2)	3	3	3	3
Wilmington, Del.	24	27	9	8	14	15	10	11
Trenton, N. J.	20	21	6	7	9	9	4	2
Manayunk	18	18	4	3	14	14	0	0
Total (See Note)	201	205	57	56	122	122	57	56

Note: Columns will not tally because not all trains listed arrive or depart Penn Center. Total Figures are number of trains actually arriving or departing Penn Center.

(1) Included in Media figures.
(2) Included in Bryn Mawr figures.
(3) Included in Paoli figures.

Over these six lines, the PC carries over 70,000 passengers each week day. Altogether, 410 week day suburban trains are operated to handle this volume of business to and from Philadelphia. Also many through trains stop at certain stations within the suburban territory providing additional service for the public. However, the through trains do not

Harrisburg, through train service doubles the suburban service to that city. Some of these trains also stop at Paoli, thereby providing additional service for that suburb. There are no through trains operated on the Chestnut Hill, West Chester or the Manayunk lines.

All suburban service from Philadelphia is through

a contract with the Southeastern Pennsylvania Transportation Authority. This contract is similar to the contract that SEPTA has with the Reading Company. This financial assistance has reduced considerably the PC's annual suburban loss. It is doubtful if there would be much service at all without SEPTA. In addition, SEPTA has in conjunction with the PC been able to provide the public with more frequent train service and coordinated bus-train service.

The following table shows the frequency of week day off hour service on the six SEPTA contract lines and the hours of service. Through trains are not counted in the frequency of service.

Line	Average Frequency In Minutes	Hours of Service
Paoli	15 to 30	5:45 AM–12:50 AM
Manayunk	60 to 90	6:05 AM–11:52 PM
Trenton	60 to 80	5:45 AM–11:55 PM
Chestnut Hill	30	6:19 AM–12:30 AM
Media—West Chester	30	5:55 AM–12:55 AM
Wilmington	60	5:44 AM–12:50 AM

In order to provide the above service, the PC operates 64 streamlined suburban coaches and 308 standard coaches. All of these cars are electric powered and their power pick up is through a pantograph on top of each car. All six of the SEPTA contract lines are electrified. The electric equipment is serviced at Philadelphia during the day and stored overnight at the following locations: Harrisburg, Paoli, Trenton, Chestnut Hill, Media, West Chester, and Wilmington. No equipment is stored at either Manayunk or Bryn Mawr. In these two cases, an equipment train departs Philadelphia early in the morning for both suburbs. These trains provide the cars for the first rush hour trains that depart for Philadelphia.

The Penn Central grosses approximately $10 million annually on their Philadelphia suburban service. As stated previously, without SEPTA support there would probably be very little suburban passenger service today. Without such service, the City of Philadelphia would be at a standstill in the movement of people over the expressways and other highways. Without such service, more expressways and parking ramps would have had to be built destroying even more land for residential or commercial use. In this writer's opinion, the SEPTA support for the PC and other rail lines has actually saved tax dollars for the entire public. In addition, SEPTA and Penn Central are continually planning and scheduling future improvements of service and facilities. Because of this thoughtful planning, and the benefits the public has already received, the future of Penn Central's Philadelphia suburban passenger service is very bright indeed.

PENN CENTRAL COMPANY
PHILADELPHIA SUBURBAN TERRITORY

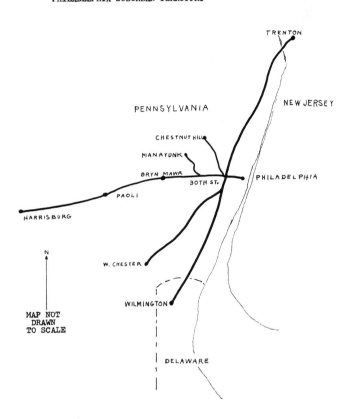

BRYN MAWR is an important suburban stop on the Harrisburg line. Here an eastbound rush hour train has stopped to pick up commuters bound for Philadelphia. (Courtesy Penn Central Company)

PRESENT DAY electrification on the Pennsylvania Railroad began with the Philadelphia-Paoli line in 1915. The electrification was expanded to include the West Chester and Wilmington lines in 1928 and to Norristown and Trenton in 1930.

Most of the Penn Central's electric MU equipment has only one pantograph for power pick up. Other roads, such as the Illinois Central, have two pantographs and alternate use either on a time or directional basis. (Courtesy Penn Central Company)

AN OVERHEAD VIEW of the two car electric MU off peak hour train at Villanova, Pennsylvania. (Courtesy Wayne P. Ellis Rail Photo Service)

A FOUR CAR MU train near Villanova, Pennsylvania on the Four Track Main Line to Harrisburg. (Courtesy Wayne P. Ellis, Rail Photo Service)

THE "OLD" and the "New" meet on the double track Chestnut Hill Line. (Courtesy Penn Central Co.)

IN LATE 1967, the City of Philadelphia purchased 20 all stainless steel coaches from General Steel Industries, Inc. for operation on the Penn Central. These new electric MU cars embodied many improvements and modifications over previous cars. For example, an extra door to speed passenger loading and unloading was provided by relocating the motorman to the left side of the vestibule. Ten of the 20 cars have experimental seating. The experimental seats consist of three different seat constructions and five different seating arrangements, all of which have two passenger seats on both sides of the aisle. The seats are upholstered with two different colors and are placed to break up the car length. These cars have a cruising speed of 85 mph. Power pick up is through a single pantograph that is located at one end of the coach. (Courtesy General Steel Industries)

THE FIRST "Silverliners" purchased by the Pennsylvania Railroad were built by the Budd Company. These cars have a seating capacity as high as 128 and are 85 feet long. The design of these cars was an outgrowth of the Budd Company's experimental coach, The Pioneer III. (Courtesy The Budd Company)

A MORNING RUSH HOUR train, No. 807, is stopping at Upsal on the Chestnut Hill line for Philadelphia bound commuters. Upsal is one of five railroad station transfer points for connections with bus routes on the Chestnut Hill line. (Courtesy Penn Central Co.)

PENN CENTRAL suburban coaches are cleaned, serviced and stored at a coach yard near 30th Street in Philadelphia. This view shows a dead head equipment train departing from the yard for a suburban terminal and its first rush hour morning run. (Courtesy Penn Central Co.)

IN A FEW INSTANCES, Class I Railroads used Gas Electrics in suburban service. This was usually done on light traffic lines. This photo shows Pennsylvania Railroad Doodlebug No. 4662 along the Pemberton Line in New Jersey. Suburban service on this line was discontinued in the late 1960's. (Courtesy Bob Lorenz)

A PENN CENTRAL suburban passenger train arriving at the 30th Street Station in Philadelphia. Passengers on New York—Washington trains may transfer to suburban trains or vica versa at this point. (Courtesy Penn Central Co.)

THROUGH TRAINS play an important part in the suburban operations of the Penn Central. Each day several through trains between New York and Pittsburgh stop at Paoli, Pennsylvania on the Harrisburg Line. Here such a train, powered by a GG1, is approaching the Paoli station and it will load several commuters at that point. (Courtesy Penn Central Company)

SUBURBANITES BETWEEN Philadelphia and Wilmington or Trenton also have a choice of certain through trains, such as the Congressionals. This is the "Midday Congressional" rounding a curve on the New York—Washington Main Line. (Courtesy Penn Central Company)

SUBURBANITES BETWEEN Philadelphia and Wilmington or Trenton, or between New York, Trenton or Philadelphia have a wider choice of accommodations than does the average commuter. Parlor Cars, such as the "Henry Knox" shown here, are operated on many of the through trains. The new "Metroliners" also include Parlor Car accommodations. The passenger car ahead of the "Henry Knox" is an all-room parlor car. Parlor cars are not handled in regular commuter trains on the Penn Central. (Courtesy Penn Central Company)

PENNSYLVANIA-READING SEASHORE LINES
SOUTHERN NEW JERSEY SUBURBAN TERRITORY

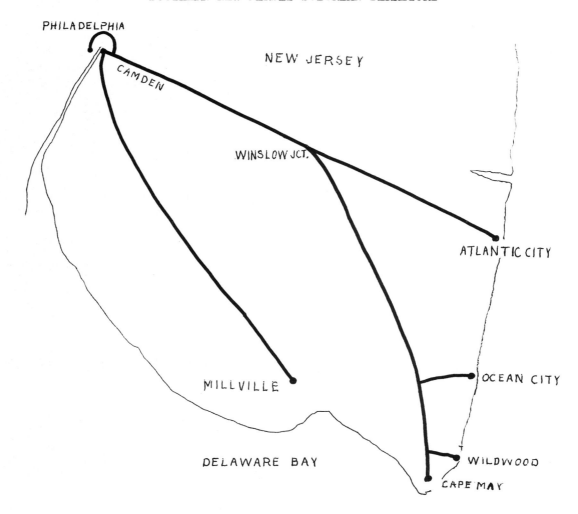

PHILADELPHIA

NEW JERSEY

CAMDEN

WINSLOW JCT.

ATLANTIC CITY

MILLVILLE

OCEAN CITY

DELAWARE BAY

WILDWOOD

CAPE MAY

The Pennsylvania-Reading Seashore Lines

The Pennsylvania-Reading Seashore Lines serve the Southern New Jersey suburbs of Philadelphia with a limited service. The Company operates trains from Philadelphia to Atlantic City, a distance of 69 miles; to Cape May, a distance of 90 miles; and to Ocean City, a distance of 78 miles. The P-RSL also operates passenger service between Camden and Millville, a distance of 40.4 miles.

The Pennsylvania-Reading Seashore lines was formed on June 25, 1933, by a merger of the West Jersey and Seashore Railroad and the Atlantic City Railroad. These two lines were a lessee of the Pennsylvania Railroad and a subsidiary of the Reading Company respectively. The Penn Central owns 66.7% of the P-RSL, while the Reading owns 33.3% of the stock in the merged property. The properties were combined because of the sharp decline in passenger and freight business during the depression.

The heaviest passenger operation is the Philadelphia—Atlantic City run. In this case, there are four trains operated in each direction. From Philadelphia, there is one non rush hour train departing in the morning. The other three are rush hour trains departing between 4:45 P.M. and 5:35 P.M. From Atlantic City, there are three rush hour trains arriving at Philadelphia from 7:20 A.M. until 8:47 A.M. The single non rush hour train departs Atlantic City in the mid-afternoon. Average running time on this line is approximately 1 hour and 40 minutes.

The rush hour and off hour trains are equipped with RDC-1's, except for the first train from Atlantic City in the morning and the last train back at night which is powered by a diesel road switcher and equipped with standard coaches.

Saturday and Sunday service consists of two trains in each direction. These trains are equipped with RDC-1's.

On the line to Ocean City and Cape May, the P-RSL operates but one rush hour train to Philadelphia in the morning and to suburbia in the evening. This train departs Philadelphia with 2 RDC-1's. Upon arrival at Tuckahoe, the rear car is detached and operates over a branch to Ocean City. The other car then proceeds to Wildwood Junction. At that point, the train operates over the four mile branch to Wildwood. Upon arrival, Wildwood passengers are discharged, and then the train returns to the main line at Wildwood Junction. From there it proceeds over the final 8 miles of its run to Cape May. The reverse operation takes place for the morning rush hour run to Philadelphia. This train operation illustrates quite clearly the advantages of Rail Diesel Cars. Just think of the switching, back up operation, and the extra time that would be required for this run with the use of conventional equipment.

The average running time for the Philly-Cape May run in both directions is 2 hours, 30 minutes. There is no Saturday or Sunday service.

The third suburban operation on the P-RSL is the Camden-Millville run. In this case, the Company operates two rush hour trains to Camden in the morning; and two from Camden in the evening. These trains are equipped with one RDC-1 each,

AT ONE TIME, there was an extensive suburban train operation on the Pennsylvania Reading Seashore lines. The electric operation between Atlantic City and Newfield was discontinued in 1931, but the electric service to Millville was continued until 1949. This photo shows a five car P-RSL electric train at Gloucested, New Jersey in 1946. (Courtesy Bob Lorenz)

and operate Monday through Friday. There is no Saturday or Sunday service.

The P-RSL carries approximately 700 week day riders and grosses $160,000 annually on its passenger operations. However this is not enough to off set the annual passenger loss of $1,250,000. Thus condition, and light density freight traffic has kept the road in very poor financial condition. It could be said that the P-RSL is another case of a railroad company subsidizing the public.

CONVENTIONAL TRAINS on the Pennsylvania Reading Seashore Lines are powered by road switchers. Here PRSL Baldwin No. 6005 is passing Brown Tower at Camden, New Jersey with three Reading Company standard coaches. This particular unit is in green livery. (Courtesy Wayne P. Ellis, Rail Photo Service)

THE PENNSYLVANIA-READING SEASHORE LINES leased both motive power and passenger equipment from its parents, the Pennsy and the Reading. The K 4 handled most of the Seashore trains until the PRSL purchased a small fleet of Baldwin Road switchers. Then steam operations were restricted to peak summer travel until more diesels and the RDC's arrived on the property. Prior to 1955, it was not uncommon to see Pennsy or Reading steam or diesel power on the head end of either regular or extra passenger trains with a mixed consist of Pennsy, Reading and PRSL coaches. The passenger revenue in 1954 for the PRSL was $2,018,614. If one compares this figure with the annual revenue of recent years, it shows up to be a real sharp decline. One can easily see the reason for one car RDC trains and for only one conventional train left on the PRSL in 1969. This PRSL train at Philly is equipped with PRR power and coaches. (Courtesy Bob Lorenz)

UPON DELIVERY of the Rail Diesel Cars, the Pennsylvania Reading Seashore Lines coupled 10 of the cars together for publicity photos. Today, nearly all P-RSL passenger trains are handled by RDC's. (Courtesy the Budd Company)

THE NORMAL CONSIST OF Pennsylvania–Reading Seashore RDC trains is two or three cars. This three car commuter run is rolling into Haddonfield, New Jersey. (Courtesy Wayne P. Ellis, Rail Photo Service)

Chapter 5

WASHINGTON-BALTIMORE, PITTSBURGH AND CLEVELAND

The Baltimore and Ohio Railroad

The B&O serves commuters on three routes in the Eastern United States: Baltimore-Washington, Washington-Brunswick and Martinsburg, West Virginia and Pittsburgh, Pa., and Versailles. The B&O grosses approximately $520,000 annually on these services, but unfortunately loses approximately $595,000 every year. It is another case of a railroad subsidizing the public.

All three routes are equipped with RDC-1's and 2's. See Roster of B&O Budd RDC Cars. 12 RDC's are used in the Washington Area Service and 5 in the Pittsburgh Area. See table on RDC Operation.

The Washington-Baltimore Service, a distance of 37 miles, is made up of almost entirely rush hour service with a total of 5 trains in each direction. These 10 trains carry 100 week day Baltimore revenue passengers and 720 week day Washington passengers. The off hour operation is the morning and afternoon Capital Limited connection between Washington and Baltimore. Week end service is provided by this train and a pair of rush hour trains to and from Washington, for a total of 2 trains in each direction.

During the year 1968, the B&O experimented with snack bars on some rush hour trains on the Baltimore-Washington runs. However, because of the mounting deficit, these were discontinued. In addition, two daily trains in each direction between Baltimore and Washington were discontinued. Average patronage on the two eastbound runs was 3 and 7 per trip. On the westbound runs, the average was 6 and 10 per trip. These trains were operated during the mid-day and late evening hours.

The B&O operates 3 week day rush hour trains in each direction west of Washington. Two trains operate from and to Brunswick, while one operates to and from Martinsburg. Martinsburg is located 73 miles west of Washington. These six trains carry approximately 930 passengers daily. Although these operations are limited in scope, the service is supplemented by four through trains in each direction that stop at Martinsburg, Harpers Ferry and Brunswick. Three of the trains also stop at Rockville. Therefore, the commuter living in Brunswick, Maryland has a choice of six trains in each direction Mondays through Fridays. None of the commuter trains operate on week ends.

Despite the rapid decline in the off hour patronage, the rush hour service has been experiencing some traffic growth. However, this growth has not been enough to off set a substantial loss of $525,000 annually.

The third part of the B&O's suburban service is the Pittsburgh, Pennsylvania-Versailles Run, a dis-

BALTIMORE & OHIO RAILROAD

Map of Baltimore-Washington Suburban Territory

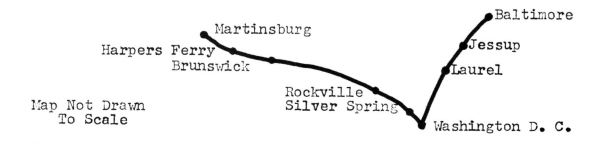

Map Not Drawn
To Scale

tance of 18 miles. This service is actually the largest of the commuter operations, yet only 5 cars are used for 14 week day runs. The run also loses the least amount of money, $70,000 annually. This shows what a higher patronage and a more efficient utilization of equipment will do to the Profit and Loss Figure. The B&O carries 1300 passengers on this route each week day, and operates three rush hour and four off hour trains in each direction.

During the morning rush hours, two trains are dispatched to Pittsburgh from Versailles and one train from McKeesport. These three trains arrive at Pittsburgh between 7:40 A.M. and 8:50 A.M. Three more westbound trains are dispatched from Mc-Keesport. These trains provide mid morning, early and late afternoon service to Pittsburgh. The last westbound train of the day is dispatched from Versailles shortly after 5 P.M.

The Eastbound off hour service is provided by two morning trains, and an early and late afternoon train (a total of four) to McKeesport. The rush hour service provides three eastbound trains departing at 4:40 P.M., 5:20 P.M. and 6:00 P.M. These trains operate through to Versailles.

Saturday service consists of four trains in each direction between Pittsburgh and McKeesport. These trains provide morning, noon and afternoon service. One of the above four trains operates from Versailles in the morning and to Versailles in the evening. There is no Sunday service.

B&O suburban service arrives and departs at the B&O Station in Pittsburgh. This is different from the through train operations that use the Pittsburgh and Lake Erie Railroad Station, as they use the P&LE main line in order to avoid the steeper B&O grades.

Although the B&O suburban operations are small compared to some of the larger roads, the service provides the only all weather passenger transportation to many suburban communities. No doubt the service could be expanded, but at this time the B&O does not have the financial resources to invest in an expansion program. However, the B&O is to be commended for providing clean, modern equipment for their service even though it is operating at a substantial loss. It is another case, where highway funds could be used more effectively for moving people by rail instead of expanding the Super Highway System.

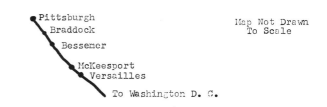

BALTIMORE & OHIO RAILROAD

Map of Pittsburgh Suburban Territory

Pittsburgh
Braddock
Bessemer
McKeesport
Versailles
To Washington D. C.

Map Not Drawn
To Scale

A HEAVY BALTIMORE & OHIO P-7A Pacific No. 5319 is heading up a morning commuter run of 1939, and is about ready to leave Washintgon, D.C. for Baltimore, Maryland. (Courtesy W. G. Fancher, Rail Photo Service)

The Pittsburgh and Lake Erie Railroad

The Pittsburgh and Lake Erie operates a suburban service north of Pittsburgh to College, Pennsylvania, a distance of 31.2 miles. The P&LE operates a single rush hour train to Pittsburgh in the morning, and to College in the evening. This train is operated on a daily except Saturday and Sunday basis.

Normally, the commuter train consists of an EMD GP-7 and 4 standard coaches. Altogether, the P&LE maintains 6 standard coaches for the suburban and/or extra service.

Although the service is very limited, the trains do provide the only all weather transportation to Northern Pittsburgh suburbia.

Rev: 1-9-69

RDC OPERATION

BALTIMORE – WASHINGTON

Weekdays

Trains	111-150-171-152	One RDC-1 and one RDC-2(1970)
Trains	161-174	Two RDC-1
Trains	106-105	One RDC-2(1951) (off No. 52)
Trains	131-108	One RDC-2(1972)

(Use 2nd unit off Train 52 when additional unit required on Trains 106-105).

Saturdays – Sundays – Holidays

| Trains | 161-106-105-108 | One RDC-2(1970) |

(When 2nd unit required on Trains 106-105, extra RDC-1 should deadhead on Train 161, and return deadhead on Train 108).

MARTINSBURG – BRUNSWICK – WASHINGTON

Train	38	One RDC-1
Train	52)	(One RDC-1 from Martinsburg plus
	)	(One RDC-2 from Brunswick
Trains	40-39	Three RDC-1
Train	37)	(One RDC-1 (off No. 52) to Martinsburg.
	)	(One RDC-2(1951) (off No. 105) to Brunswick.
Train	51	One RDC-1

VERSAILLES – McKEESPORT – PITTSBURGH

Except Saturdays – Sundays – Holidays

| Trains | 547-548 | Two RDC-1 and one RDC-2 |

561-562-563-564-)	
565-566-567-568-)	Two RDC-1
569-570-571-572-)	

Saturdays only

| Trains | 547-564-565-566-) | One RDC-1 |
| | 567-568-569-548-) | |

96

A B&O COMMUTER TRAIN crossing the Thomas Viaduct near Relay, Maryland. Relay is approximately 7 miles from Baltimore. (Courtesy Baltimore & Ohio Railroad)

B&O COMMUTERS from the Martinsburg-Brunswick line arriving in Washington, D.C. (Courtesy Baltimore & Ohio Railroad)

AN ARTIST'S RENDITION of a B&O commuter train passing Harpers Ferry, West Virginia. (Courtesy The Budd Company)

AN INTERIOR VIEW of a B&O RDC-2 which was once equipped with kitchen and booths for meal and bar service. Now these cars have 24 reclining seats and 24 bench seats. (Courtesy Baltimore & Ohio Railroad)

B&O COMMUTER train No. 52 on the Martinsburg-Washington run. This train currently operates with two cars. (Courtesy Baltimore & Ohio Railroad)

DURING THE SUMMER OF 1968, the B&O experimented with Bar Service on their Washington Commuter Service. However, the service was discontinued on October 7, 1968 because of the mounting deficit. (Courtesy Baltimore & Ohio Railroad)

THE BALTIMORE & OHIO once operated a commuter service in three directions from Pittsburgh, in both directions on the Main Line and the line to Cincinnati. Through trains played a large part in the service to the growing Pittsburgh suburbia for many decades. However, as with many other suburban services, the automobile either single handedly or with the depression killed many of the services for good. B&O heavy Pacific No. 5241 is getting under way from the Pittsburgh Station with a heavy load of evening commuters bound for suburbia. The train itself is enroute to Cincinnati. (Courtesy G. Grabill, Jr., Rail Photo Service)

A NUMBER OF B&O THROUGH TRAINS stop at certain stations within the Washington, D. C. suburban territory. The National Limited was one such train before its discontinuance. The short train, which was later combined with C&O's George Washington on the St. Louis Run, is shown here stopping at Harpers Ferry for passengers. (Courtesy Bob Lorenz)

ONE AND TWO CAR RDC trains are the rule of thumb on the Pittsburgh-Versailles suburban runs. Saturdays trains usually have one car, while some week day trains have three cars. This photo was taken during a rainy day. Rain, sleet and snow bring many drivers to the suburban trains while the bad weather lasts-foul weather friends. When they get to the railroad station and board the train, they grumble because the railroad company has not provided enough seats. Bad weather has caused patronage to double and even triple on some runs around North America. The railroads cannot be expected to maintain double the number of seats for the foul weather friends. Another reason for some sort of public support for suburban operations. (Courtesy Bob Lorenz)

THE PITTSBURGH AND LAKE ERIE RAILROAD passenger service is limited to a single suburban run today (1969), but the road once operated an extensive service between Pittsburgh and Youngstown, Ohio; a distance of only 64.9 miles. In 1954, for example the road operated 7 daily trains in each direction between the above two points; plus 3 westbound and 4 eastbound rush hour commuter trains between Pittsburgh and College. The Youngstown trains provided commuter service beyond College, and in conjunction with the Erie and the B&O, businessman commuter service between Cleveland and Pittsburgh. These trains offered reclining seat coaches and P&LE, Erie and B&O operated Parlor-Dining Cars for the 132 mile commuter run. Today there is no direct train service on the Cleveland-Pittsburgh run with a freight only gap between College and Youngstown. However, there has been a proposal for a study of traffic potential for a high speed corridor service between the two cities.

This photo shows P&LE Pacific No. 9233 charging out of New Castle, Pennsylvania. The steamer was built by Alco in 1918, class K-4b, and is equipped with a trailer booster. The parallel tracks belong to the B&O. (Courtesy S. K. Bolton, Jr. Rail Photo Service)

CLEVELAND, OHIO

The Erie Lackawanna Railroad

The Erie Lackawanna operates a single rush hour suburban train in each direction between Cleveland and Youngstown, Ohio, a distance of 66.2 miles. This train stops at all suburbs in the Cleveland area and operates to Cleveland in the morning, and departs for Youngstown after 5 P.M. Each train carrys approximately 300 week day passengers, for a total of 600 riders for each round trip.

The Erie Lackawanna Cleveland service is the only rail suburban transportation in the State of Ohio.

THE ERIE RAILROAD (Now Erie Lackawanna) once operated, in each direction, six daily trains between Cleveland and Youngstown. Two of these in each direction were rush hour commuter runs and originated and terminated at Youngstown. The other four were operated with the P&LE for the Cleveland-Pittsburgh service. This photo shows one of the Cleveland-Pittsburgh trains at Youngstown shortly after diesels arrived on the property. Today, there is but one train between Cleveland and Youngstown—a rush hour run in each direction. The present train is equipped with one E-8 and 6 reclining seat streamlined coaches. Although the service is modern and clean, it is a far cry from the service of the early 1950's with six passenger trains in each direction. (Courtesy W. G. Fancher, Rail Photo Service)

Chapter 6
CHICAGO

Chicago and North Western Railway

If there ever was a success story in railroading, it has been the C&NW's management team's ability to make a profit on their suburban operations. At one time, in fact for decades, the C&NW had a money losing suburban operation—as most other railroads continue to do so today. The railway's patronage, passenger miles and net income have been increasing every year since 1962. How is it that the C&NW has been able to do this?

The North Western has the largest suburban operation on three routes from Chicago. The Road carries approximately 90,000 daily passengers. The three routes extend from Chicago to Kenosha, Wisconsin, a distance of 51.6 miles; from Chicago to Harvard, 63.1 miles; the Lake Geneva Branch, 71.0 miles from Chicago and from Chicago to Geneva, 35.5 miles. Nearly 200 trains operate over the three lines providing frequent rush hour service and hourly service at other times during the day.

In 1956, the C&NW ran a suburban service with cars dating back to 1910 and steam locomotives. Very few cars were air conditioned and most of the equipment was not fit to run, but they were in service. About the only thing that could be said was that the trains provided nostalgia for the rail fan. The 4-6-2's and 4-6-0's were nice too look at, but did little for clean and profitable service.

The suburban service was large and important. In fact, it was too big to die. The usual path would have led the railroad to frequent applications for a few train discontinuances here and there in an attempt to keep costs down. Each step would have driven more passengers away. The future looked bleak, especially with new expressways being built. The management took a long hard look at this situation. The Railroad as a whole was in poor shape and the suburban service only added to its woes. The management's study of the commuter service revealed that a profit potential existed, but it could not be achieved with the 1910 style of operation. A daring new plan was developed.

This plan involved replacing all old cars with 200 new double deck, push pull passenger cars. Today, this fleet has increased in size with orders for new cars occuring nearly every year. The total number in 1969 is 275 with 64 of those cars equipped with a cab compartment and remote control apparatus for operating diesel locomotives on the other end of the push pull train.

These push pull trains always operate with the locomotive headed out from Chicago. On inbound runs, the motive power is at the rear pushing. Outbound, they pull the train in the conventional manner. When the locomotive is pushing from the rear, the engine crew controls the train from a cab in the leading car. This cab is equipped with the same controls and safety devices that are in the cab of the locomotive.

The biggest advantage in the use of push pull trains is the elimination of much switching of trains and locomotives, with the consequent saving of time and switching costs. The Chicago Terminal is a stub terminal. When a conventional train arrives at Chicago, the locomotive is at the wrong end for efficient return movement. Either the train must back out or another locomotive must be switched to the other end. A separate crewman must handle the back-up brake control when trains are backed to the yards for servicing. During the days of conventional suburban service, if a train was backed to the suburbs for another run during the rush period, the entire train of cars was taken along because there wasn't sufficient time to switch out the cars that were not needed. However, on an inbound push pull train, if it is going to make an outbound trip, the engineer and fireman simply transfer to the other end, and the locomotive pulls the train to the suburbs or to the servicing yards. Whatever number of cars that are not needed on this return movement are disconnected and left in the terminal for use on other trains or for subsequent servicing.

The push pull coaches are built to be as trouble free as possible. The cars are electrically heated or cooled, and they receive their electric power from a special electric generator on the diesel locomotive. Thus, virtually all the underbody hardware has been eliminated. There are no steam pipes that can leak or freeze in the winter or no noisy generators for lights and air conditioning. This improvement has reduced the weight of such double deck cars by about 10 tons when compared to earlier models. This type of operation has resulted in a vast cost reduction for the North Western without sacrificing passenger comfort—in fact, it has improved passen-

BESIDES A FLEET of Ten wheelers, and Pacifics, the C&NW also operated a number of Atlantics in suburban service. This Class "D" is equipped with a Stenphenson valve gear and was one of a few C&NW steamers that were oil burners. (Courtesy Chicago & North Western Ry.)

ger comfort.

Prior to the improvement program, mid-day and evening service on the three lines was not very good. It was often several hours between trains. The North Western management realized that the best equipment in the world will not earn a nickel if there are no trains. Therefore, all non rush hour service was restored to one hour frequency. The result was increased patronage and improved utilization of equipment. But there was more work to be done. The next step taken was a vast advertising program on the radio, TV and newspapers. Radio advertisements were aimed at the motorist, right when he was stuck in a traffic jam on the free way. Traffic jams that were never supposed to happen. In addition, the C&NW pointed out with cost figures that it was cheaper to commute by train then it was to drive. The result was still more increased patronage, which is still happening and the suburban operations have been in the black since 1963. The Railroad is currently grossing about $19 million and nets about $2½ million annually.

In addition to the double decker coaches, the C&NW operates a number of lounge cars in certain trains providing snack and beverage service in the evening, and coffee and rolls in the morning.

The operations during the rush hour for the three lines is immense. From 6 A.M. to 9 A.M., there are 15 trains arriving at Chicago from the North Line, 20 trains from the Northwest Line, and 15 trains from the West Line for a total of 50 trains. Some of these trains arrive simultaneously from the various districts. In the evening from 4 P.M. until 6:30 P.M., there are 13 trains departing on the North Line, 17 trains on the Northwest Line and 11 trains on the West Line for a total of 41 trains. This count of trains does not include through trains, such as the Peninsula 400, switching moves of passenger equipment or empty trains arriving for loading or departing for the yards. One can stand on the Lake Street Elevated Station Platform above the C&NW Terminal (The two stations are physically connected.) to watch this activity. Just think of the job that the Lake Street Tower Operator has in controlling the switches at the entrance to the North Western Terminal.

The Chicago and North Western Management is to be complemented for providing one of the outstanding suburban train service to be found anywhere in the world.

THE CHICAGO & NORTH WESTERN RAILWAY operated a large fleet of Pacific type steam locomotives in suburban service prior to 1956. Many of these locomotives that were assigned permanently to suburban service had pilots mounted on the tanks for back up running. Another unique feature of C&NW steam power was the addition of a red mars light mounted on top of the smoke box. This photo was taken during the C&NW's celebration of its first 100 years in operation in 1949. (Courtesy Bob Lorenz)

PRIOR TO COMPLETE MODERNIZATION and the Push Pull streamliners, The C&NW operated F-M 1600 HP "Baby Trainmasters" and EMD GP and SD units to power suburban trains. Here the 1691 is arriving at Clybourn with a morning rush hour train. (Courtesy Chicago & North Western Ry.)

AN EARLY AFTERNOON rush hour train departing Chicago on the Northwest Line. Notice that the traffic on the parallel expressway is already quite heavy. (Courtesy Chicago & North Western Ry.)

A MORNING RUSH HOUR Push Pull train is shown here arriving at Glen Ellyn, Illinois on the West Line. (Courtesy Chicago & North Western Ry.)

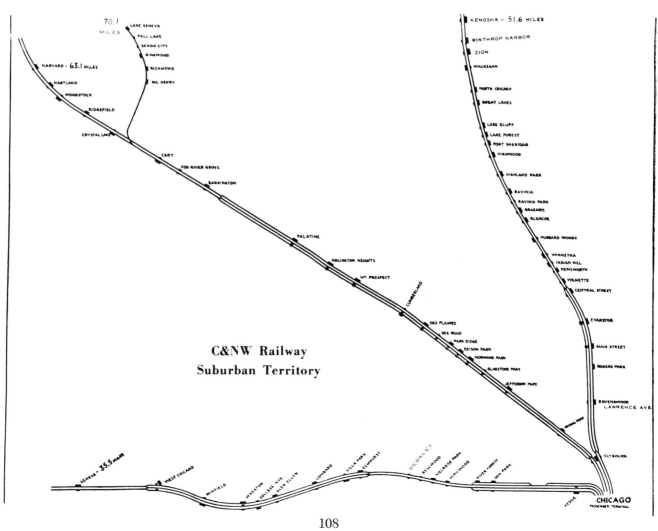

C&NW Railway
Suburban Territory

A MORNING RUSH HOUR suburban train has just arrived at the Chicago Terminal. The engineer and the fireman will now walk back to the F-7 diesel locomotive at the other end of the train, and make a fast return trip to the suburbs for another load of inbound commuters. (Courtesy Chicago & North Western Ry.)

A LAKE STREET CHICAGO Transit Authority elevated train enroute to Oak Park, Illinois. This train is made up of air conditioned rapid transit cars that were built by Pullman-Standard. The Lake Street "L" has a station directly over the C&NW's Chicago Terminal. These two facilities are now physically connected. This means that passengers arriving on C&NW trains may transfer to the "L" for fast transportation to any part of the Chicago Loop. (Courtesy Pullman-Standard)

THE C&NW has also converted a number of E-8's for commuter streamliner service. These units are generally assigned to the longer rush hour trains.

PRIOR TO THE PURCHASE of double deck commuter coaches, the C&NW experimented with three Budd RDC cars. They purchased one RDC-2 and two RDC-1's in the Spring of 1950. The Railroad operated the three cars in Chicago area suburban service until the Fall of 1957 when they were traded to the Chesapeake & Ohio for 3 streamlined coaches. The three RDC's eventually ended up on the Baltimore & Ohio. Today, only two of the three original cars remain. C&NW 9933, which became B&O 1971 was destroyed in a wreck.

The RDC is generally not very economical when operated in long trains. For example, an eight car rush hour double deck commuter streamliner can carry over 1250 passengers. Such a train is usually powered by an E-8 2250 HP diesel. To carry 1250 passengers with RDC's, one would need 13 such cars. The total horse power involved here would be 7800. That is quite a difference in fuel costs alone. In addition, more men would be required to collect tickets in the thirteen cars than would be required in the 8 car double deck train. This is one of the reasons why C&NW went double deck push pull trains, besides the fact that push pulls have most of the advantages of MU or RDC equipment. (Courtesy Chicago & North Western Ry.)

NEW $3,500,000 commuter coach service center being constructed by Chicago and North Western Railway adjacent to its main line at California Avenue, directly west of downtown Chicago. Day-to-day servicing as well as all light and heavy repairs to the railway's growing bi-level suburban coach fleet will take place at this modern facility scheduled for completion in the fall of 1969. (Courtesy C & NW Ry.)

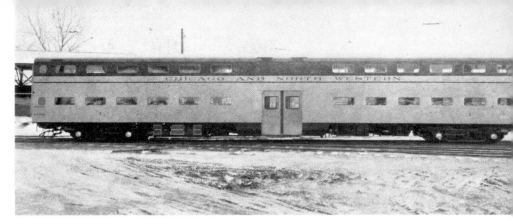

SUBURBAN COACH NO. 1 was the first car of the first order of 16 double deck coaches for the Chicago & North Western Ry. These sixteen cars were built by St. Louis Car Division of General Steel Industries in 1955 at a cost of $2,240,000. These cars have now been converted for Push Pull operation. (Courtesy General Steel Industries)

THIS PHOTO, taken from the center vestibule, shows the interior of coach No. 1. The center vestibule divides the car into two passenger compartments. Just inside the compartments are stairs on each side of the car leading to the upper gallery. On the upper level, a row of single seats line each side of the car. Seven seats on each side of the upper level are parallel to the length of the car and are counter weighted to fold against the wall when not in use. At the end of each gallery is one double seat. The cars are decorated in a light tan or buff color scheme with green rubber tile flooring. The foam rubber seats are upholstered in vinyl plastic with either red or green colored seats. The seats are of tubular stainless steel framing and are reversible. The seating capacity of these coaches is 169 passengers. All interiors of double deck cars built since 1955 have the same basic design. (Courtesy General Steel Industries)

MOST OF THE CHICAGO & NORTH WESTERN RAILWAY'S double deck suburban equipment was built by Pullman-Standard. Here is a builder's photo of a recently built car equipped with a cab for push pull operation. Coaches without cabs are identical to the car shown except that they are minus the extra cab windows, electric marker lamps, end ladders, pilot, headlights, red mars light and have a slightly higher seating capacity. (Courtesy Pullman-Standard)

AN INTERIOR VIEW of the upper level of a suburban coach built by Pullman Standard. The doors at the rear of the car lead to the engineer's side of the cab. (Courtesy Pullman-Standard)

THE C&NW was the first railroad to incorporate a commuter coach design into a long distance passenger car. This Bi-Level 400 coach is identical in exterior appearances to Pullman Standard double deck commuter cars operated on the C&NW. The only difference is the interior seating arrangement. The 400 coaches seat 96 passengers and can be operated with the commuter cars if need be.

THROUGH TRAINS on the Chicago & North Western play only a minor role in the Chicago-Milwaukee area suburban picture. The Railway operates, in each direction, a train called the "Commuter 400" during the morning rush hour. The trains are equipped with standard "400" type streamlined coaches and make the 84.2 mile Chicago-Milwaukee run in 95 minutes including stops at Racine, Kenosha and Waukegan. These trains provide commuter businessmen with arrival in either Chicago or Milwaukee after 9 A.M. For the return trip home, the Company provides an after 4:00 P.M. departure from each city. Northbound this is the Bi-Level Peninsula 400. Southbound is train No. 160, known as the "400 Streamliner." This train is equipped with standard 400 coaches, usually 4 to 5 in the consist with no head-end cars. When this photo was taken in September 1950, train 160 was sporting a brand new E-8 (the 5021A), a standard Mail & Baggage, Parlor Car with Drawing Room, 2 coaches (one in the UP color scheme) and a Baggage Tap Cafe Lounge Car (Courtesy Jim Scribbins)

THE C&NW HAS REBUILT several of its club lounge and tavern cars for use in suburban service, or for extra service on the Bi-level 400's. These cars are used in several trains on a regular basis, such as on the Chicago-Lake Geneva run. The cars, however, no longer retain their original UP style paint scheme and have been repainted to match the new suburban equipment. The cars have seating capacities varying from 36 to 46. The equipment is operated to serve sweet rolls and coffee inbound in the morning, and beverages outbound in the evening. During the Horse Racing season, the C&NW operates passenger extras to the race tracks and these cars are included in the consist along with the double deck suburban coaches. This lounge car service has been very popular and is heavily patronized by suburbanites, and is the only such service operated in the Chicago area. (Courtesy Chicago & North Western Ry.)

A PORTRAIT OF A C&NW 400 type streamliner coach. These coaches are used to equip all Chicago-Clinton, Iowa and Milwaukee, Wisconsin trains including the "Commuter 400." All coaches of this type on the C&NW have been completely rebuilt in recent years and have a slightly different paint scheme today. The black stripe is now missing and lettering is in yellow and numerals are black. Otherwise the scheme is not changed. The winged diaphrams have also been removed because of maintenance difficulties, however the coaches are equipped with standard diaphrams. These streamlined beauties were built in 1947, and because of rebuilding, they still have a high comfort index. (Courtesy Chicago & North Western Ry.)

AN INTERIOR VIEW of a 56 reclining seat 400 style streamlined coach shortly after construction by Pullman Standard in 1947. Since then, these coaches have been completely rebuilt and no longer include the hard to maintain Venetian blinds. (Courtesy Chicago & North Western Ry.)

THE C&NW PROVIDES DINER-LOUNGE service on some of the Chicago-Milwaukee trains. Suburbanites are able to make use of this equipment while traveling between Chicago and Kenosha, Racine and Milwaukee. The Company serves Continental Breakfasts in the morning and meals, snacks and beverages in the afternoon and evening on these Chicago-Milwaukee trains. Some of this equipment was built as early as 1941, but all equipment has had extensive rebuilding since then. In fact, all of the lounge cars and most of the diner lounge cars have been equipped with the electrical fixtures required to operate in the consist of suburban trains or Bi-level 400's, which use electric power instead of steam. (Courtesy Chicago & North Western Ry.)

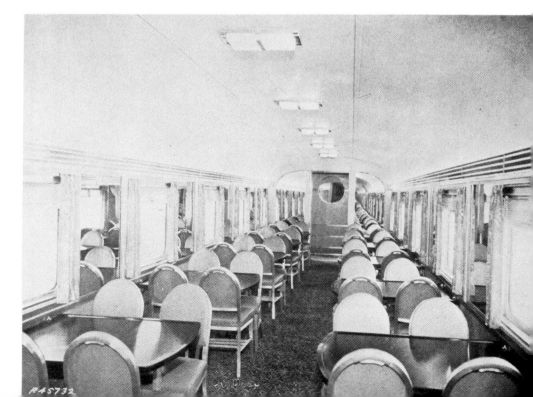

AN INTERIOR VIEW of C&NW Diner Lounge car looking toward the dining section of the car. (Courtesy Chicago & North Western Ry.)

The Milwaukee Road

The Milwaukee Road serves Suburban Districts in both the Chicago and the Milwaukee Areas.

The Chicago service includes both a North Line and a West Line from the Chicago Union Station. The North Line goes North on the First Subdivision of the Milwaukee Division to Roundout. At that point, the suburban district turns on to the Second Subdivision and continues on to Walworth, a distance of 73.5 miles. The West Line goes west on the Dubuque and Illinois Division to Elgin, a distance of 36.8 miles.

The company handles about 22,000 week day passengers. During the rush hour from 6:30 A.M. until 9:00 A.M., there are 8 Chicago arrivals on both the North Line and the West Line, for a total of 16 trains. During the evening rush hour from 4:00 P.M. to 6:00 P.M., there are 7 departures on the North Line and 6 departures on the West Line. Mid-day and evening service varies from a frequency of one to three hours on both of the lines. However, the train schedules are set up in such a way as to conveniently accomodate morning, afternoon, or evening shoppers and theatre goers. There are a total of 16 trains in each direction on both lines for a total of 64 week day runs. This reduces to 5 each way on Sundays for each line. On the North Line, most of the trains operate only to Fox Lake and a few rush hour trains operate only to and from Deerfield. On the West Line, all but two operate to Elgin. The others operate only as far as Bensenville, the location of the Milwaukee Road's Chicago area push button yard.

Milwaukee Road trains range from one car to eight cars, depending upon the time of day. It is interesting to note that one car trains are limited to 70 miles per hour rather then the usual 75 MPH. The reasoning here is the same as for caboose hops, which are usually limited to 50 MPH, the train is just too light for higher speeds.

The Milwaukee Road has gone through a considerable expense and effort to completely modernize its suburban service. All trains are push pull and use exactly the same type of operation as explained in the section on the C&NW. The Company has a total of 62 double deck stainless steel coaches, built by Budd; of which 20 cars are equipped with a control cab. The Milwaukee Road uses a fleet of FP-7's and E-9's for suburban motive power. These diesels are also equipped with an electric generator for supplying power to the train for air conditioning and lighting. In fact, the Milwaukee Road equipment is quite similar to the North Western's push pull equipment. There are some differences in window configuration and the Milwaukee Cars are stainless

steel. This equipment and modernization program has made significant strides in reducing costs while improving the quality of service for the Chicago District Suburbanites. In fact, the Company has added several trains since 1965. This effort has been successful in reducing costs and has reversed the downward trend in suburban patronage in the Chicago Area.

The Milwaukee Road also operates a commuter service between Milwaukee and Watertown, Wisconsin, a distance of 46 miles. The company operates one train in each direction daily except Saturday and Sunday. The train consists of two streamlined coaches and operates to Milwaukee in the morning and returns to Watertown in the evening. Both the outbound and inbound runs take approximately 70 minutes.

At the time of this writing, many of the through trains (to and from Minneapolis) stop at Watertown and Oconomoc. Therefore, the Milwaukee suburban passenger, who lives in one of the above towns, has a choice of 5 inbound runs and four outbound trains. These trains provide morning, noon afternoon and evening service.

Although the population of western Milwaukee Suburbia is small compared to Chicago Suburbia, the Milwaukee Road is to be commended for its service to those towns. In fact, the Milwaukee Road operates the last rail suburban service out of Milwaukee, which once included several electric railways.

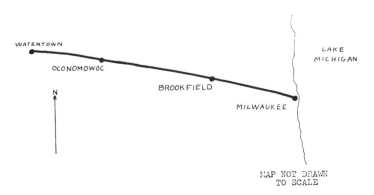

THE MILWAUKEE ROAD
MILWAUKEE SUBURBAN TERRITORY

NORMAL STEAM POWER for Milwaukee Road suburban trains was Pacific Type F-3's. Here the 162 is shown leaving Bensenville with train No. 242 enroute to Chicago on September 16, 1950. (Courtesy Jim Scribbins)

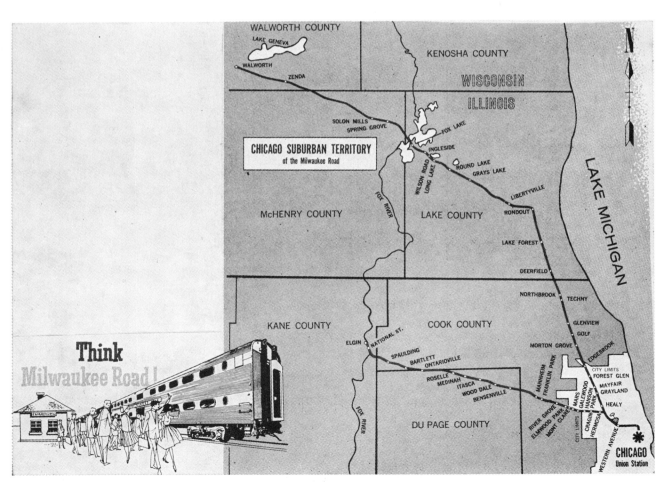

AS WITH ALL CHANGE OVERS from steam to diesel, many heavy and/or high speed steam locomotives began to get tasks that they were rarely assigned to before. Near the end of steam on the Milwaukee Road, Class F-6-A's (Straight running boards and air pumps on pilot as compared to F-6.) Hudsons were assigned to commuter trains. Here the 143 is rolling west with train No. 155 (East of Libertyville) enroute to Fox Lake on June 23, 1954. (Courtesy Jim Scribbins)

PRIOR to the complete modernization of the Milwaukee Road suburban service, the Company used road switchers for suburban train motive power. Here a GP-9, painted in the Union Pacific color scheme, approaches the Glenview station with a conventional train. (Courtesy The Milwaukee Road)

IN THE EARLY 1960's, when the first suburban double deck coaches and the new E-9's were delivered, a special train was made up for display at the various depots in the suburban territory. That train is shown here on display at the Glenview station. Note the sign describing the new equipment near the door of the second coach. (Courtesy The Milwaukee Road)

A MILWAUKEE ROAD commuter train at suburban Deerfield, Illinois. (Courtesy The Milwaukee Road)

THE MILWAUKEE ROAD passenger station at Glenview, Illinois. (Courtesy The Milwaukee Road)

MILWAUKEE ROAD suburban passenger service has been completely modernized since January of 1965, all trains on its suburban lines to the north and west of Chicago being made up completely of stainless steel, double deck coaches, such as shown here. With this new equipment the railroad began operating eleven additional suburban trains and stepped up the schedules of 18 others on March 22, 1965. (Courtesy The Milwaukee Road)

PRIOR TO COMPLETE PUSH PULL OPERATION, The Milwaukee Road operated their new stainless steel coaches in the conventional manner. Here the 95A is approaching the station at Northbrook, Illinois with a four car rush hour train enroute to Chicago. (Courtesy The Milwaukee Road)

A PORTRAIT OF A DOUBLE DECK stainless steel suburban coach built by the Budd Company for the Milwaukee Road. The Milwaukee Road owns 62 of these very attractive cars. This coach, equipped with a cab for push pull operation, has a seating capacity of 156 passengers. Coaches without cabs seat 162 passengers. (Courtesy the Milwaukeen Road)

BI-LEVEL COACHES AND DIESEL LOCOMOTIVES assigned to Milwaukee Road suburban passenger service pictured at Elgin, Ill., on a Sunday evening as the equipment stands ready for the Monday morning rush hour.

Although Elgin is the western terminus of the railroad's west suburban line, the Milwaukee road main line continues westward to Omaha, Neb., and Kansas City, Mo. (Courtesy The Milwaukee Road)

A MODERN MILWAUKEE ROAD commuter train at suburban Glenview, Illinois. (Courtesy The Milwaukee Road)

BETWEEN WATERTOWN AND MILWAUKEE operates the only suburban train serving the Wisconsin metropolis: Milwaukee Road No. 12 and 23 (LaCrosse Division). The trains are well known locally, though un-officially, as the "Cannon Ball." Though the train has a number of loyal riders who agreed several years ago to pay higher fares to keep the train running, some patronage has been lost to freeways and special buses.

When the conductor of the past nine years retired in March, 1969, the event received front page coverage with photos in the Sunday edition of the local newspaper.

Normal consist of 12 and 23 is an FP 7 pulling two coaches originally constructed for the Hiawatha of 1942. Unfortunately, the Southeastern Wisconsin Regional Planning Commission favors more freeways, including special bus expressways to move commuters.

This photo shows No. 12 arriving at Hartland, Wisconsin on a sunny Spring morning in April, 1968. (Courtesy Jim Scribbins)

ALTHOUGH THE BURLINGTON was quick to dieselize its through passenger trains, steam was still to be found in great abundance in the suburban territory in 1948 and 1949. Here the 2949, a 4-6-2 Pacific, charges westbound with a six car early rush hour train near La Grange, Illinois on August 22, 1949. (Courtesy Jim Scribbins)

The Burlington Route

The Burlington Route has one of the most modern suburban passenger operations in the World between the Chicago Union Station and Aurora, Illinois; a distance of 38.0 miles. The Company has always taken care to pamper its passengers, both suburban and through. Except for the combination Power and Coach cars, all equipment in the suburban service is double deck stainless steel coaches built by the Budd Company. The Burlington was the first railroad to use this bi-level design, which has now spread to three other Chicago lines and a West Coast railroad for both through and suburban service.

The Company first put this type of car in service in the late 1940's. At that time, they also air-conditioned all other standard coaches that were kept in use. These standard cars were kept in good running condition until the Burlington replaced all of them with new double deck cars, that were built by Budd in the early 1960's. The company now has a total of 88 double deck cars with six of the new cars equipped with a cab for push-pull operation. However, the Railroad uses this type of operation for only mid-day and evening runs, and certain other rush hour trains.

The Burlington suburban trains draw their power for air conditioning and lighting from generators installed in the combination power-coach cars.

The Company services the suburban equipment during the day at the 14th Street Coach Yard, located just south of the Union Station in Chicago. At night, most of the equipment is stored at Aurora, Illinois where it is cleaned and readied for the next day's runs.

The train operations include 31 eastbound runs and 32 west bound runs. The non-rush hour frequency varies from 50 minutes to 2 Hours and 20 minutes. During the rush hour from 6:30 A.M. to 9:00 A.M., there are 18 arrivals in Chicago, with many of the trains only two minutes apart. During the evening from 4:00 P.M. to 6:00 P.M., there are 16

OPEN END COACHES were used in Burlington Suburban service until 1948, when the first double deck stainless steel suburban coaches were purchased from the Budd Company. At that time, the open end cars were retired and all remaining standard coaches were rebuilt and air conditioned. (Courtesy Bob Lorenz)

departures, with many trains on two or three minute headways. Many of the rush hour trains are expresses and do not stop at every station. The average running time between Chicago and Aurora varies from 50 to 75 minutes.

All trains are powered by EMD E/8's or E/9's. These locomotives operate in power pools which find them in suburban service one day and Denver the next. All motive power is equipped with cab signals for operation on the Chicago-Aurora triple track speedway. This section of the railroad is CTC Territory and all three tracks are signaled for operation in either direction. All trains, of course, are radio equipped.

At the present time, the Burlington is handling over 19,000 week-day passengers. This results in a gross revenue of over $5.2 million per year. In 1958, the gross revenue of the suburban operations was $3.7 million. Despite the gradual increase in revenues over the past ten years, costs have increased at a faster rate. Although the operation has not been a severe financial drain on the Company, the service has generally operated on a marginal basis. However, the population along the line to Aurora is increasing at a rapid rate. The railroad physical plant is in excellent shape and it can handle more passengers with little or no expansion. With this present traffic growth (which is expected to continue) and if costs do not continue to pace the increased patronage, hopefully the Railroad will be able to operate a suburban service that will contribute significantly to the profit picture.

A MORNING BURLINGTON ROUTE rush hour suburban train enroute to Chicago on the center track of the triple track speed way. (Courtesy The Burlington Route)

A MID-MORNING PUSH PULL TRAIN enroute to Chicago has stopped at Hinsdale, Illinois to take on passengers. (Courtesy The Burlington Route)

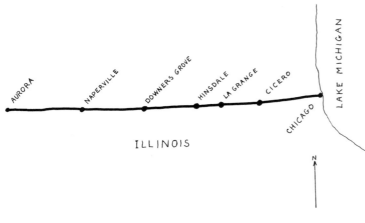

THE BURLINGTON ROUTE

CHICAGO SUBURBAN TERRITORY

AURORA   NAPERVILLE   DOWNERS GROVE   HINSDALE   LA GRANGE   CICERO   CHICAGO   LAKE MICHIGAN

ILLINOIS

N

MAP NOT DRAWN
TO SCALE

A PUSH PULL TRAIN arriving at Chicago. (Courtesy The Burlington Route)

A WESTBOUND PUSH PULL TRAIN, en route to Aurora, is shown here between Lisle and Naperville, Illinois on the Chicago and Aurora Subdivision of the Chicago Division. (Courtesy The Burlington Route)

THE BURLINGTON ROUTE also purchased their suburban coaches from the Budd Company. However, the CB&Q's equipment is slightly different from the double deck cars operated on the Milwaukee Road and the Rock Island. For example, the cab control cars do not include permanent electric marker lamps. Instead, the "Q" uses portable electric markers as shown in the photo. Although they are small, they do provide a very bright light. In addition, the equipment uses steam for heating. This means the equipment could be used with conventional passenger equipment. However, it is very seldom that these cars venture outside the suburban territory. (Courtesy The Burlington Route)

The Rock Island Railroad

The Rock Island Railroad operates an extensive suburban service between Chicago and Southwestern suburbs. The Company grosses over $4 million annually and carries over 26,000 week day riders. The Road operates two suburban lines, one known as the Main Line between Chicago and Joliet, a distance of 40.2 miles; and the other known as the Suburban Branch, which leaves the Main Line at Gresham Junction and extends to Blue Island. Blue Island is 16.4 miles from Chicago. The Company operates at total of 77 trains every week day over the two lines.

The Company operates 13 trains each way between Chicago and Joliet. Of these 5 arrive at Chicago between 6:00 A.M. and 9:00 A.M., and 5 depart between 4:00 P.M. and 7:00 P.M. The other trains operate throughout the day until mid-night with frequencies of 2 to 3 hours. On the Suburban Branch to Blue Island, there are 12 arrivals at Chicago from 6:00 A.M. to 9:00 A.M. and 11 departures from 4:00 P.M. to 7:00 P.M. There are a total 26 arrivals and 25 departures at Chicago for the Suburban Branch each week day. These trains operate throughout the day at one to two hour frequencies. On Saturdays, the Company operates 9 trains in each direction on the Main Line; and 14 eastbound trains and 13 westbound trains on the Suburban Branch. On Sunday, the service frequency reduces to 6 each way on the Main Line, and 8 eastbounds and 9 westbounds on the Suburban Branch.

During the past few years, the Rock Island has embarked on a suburban service improvement program. However, it has not progressed as fast as the management has desired because of financial problems. At the present time, the Rock Island has 117 coaches in suburban service. 20 of these are streamlined air conditioned coaches. 20 are double deck Budd built push pull cars of which 5 are equipped with a cab for the push pull operation. The other 77 cars are standard coaches. These cars will be replaced as rapidly as possible, funds permitting. Meanwhile, the newer cars have improved the quality of service and have provided the Company with lower maintenance costs.

Suburban coach yards are located at Blue Island and Joliet. During the day, the cars are serviced in the La Salle Street Station shed, and stored overnight at Blue Island and Joliet to await their morning runs to Chicago. A few locomotives stay overnight at Joliet and are serviced at the diesel shed. All others are serviced at the Blue Island Roundhouse.

The Rock Island, in addition to building and purchasing new suburban passenger equipment, has also been rebuilding old stations or building new ones as funds permit. The new depots have usually been contemporary brick ranch type structures. They normally have a 600-square foot waiting room that is furnished with modern fiberglass furniture. The interiors are painted pastel colors and use fluorescent lighting. Such new depots cost the Rock Island over $20,000 each to construct.

The population of the Rock Island Suburban area is expanding. The Southwest Expressway, recently completed, has not been able to efficiently handle all the traffic that has been developing. The Rock Island is in a very strategic position for the handling of suburban passengers to and from Chicago. If the Rock Island will not have to compete with the Chicago Transit Authority Transportation System to the southwest, the Company will be able to look forward to increased patronage and, hopefully, a substantial contribution to the Profit Figure.

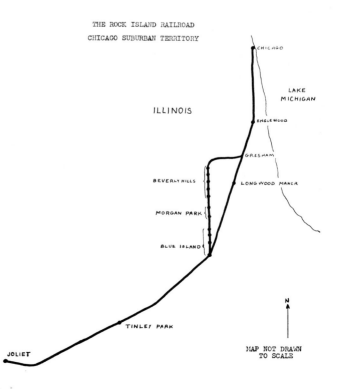

THE ROCK ISLAND RAILROAD
CHICAGO SUBURBAN TERRITORY

MAP NOT DRAWN
TO SCALE

A ROCK ISLAND Surburban train passing the suburban coach yard south of the La Salle Street Station—Chicago during the days of steam. Today this yard is no longer used as suburban equipment is stored and serviced within the station itself. (Courtesy Bob Lorenz)

THE TIME IS 1948, and steam still rules on the Rock Island. The RI Pacific No. 942 is arriving at Chicago with a seven car express train from Blue Island, as New York Central steamer No. 4713 is backing from the La Salle Street Station to the Engine terminal to be turned and serviced for another passenger run. (Courtesy W. G. Fancher, Rail Photo Service)

DURING THE DAYS OF STEAM, the Rock Island employed type P-33 Pacifics in suburban service. Here the 901 departs Englewood for Joliet with a non rush hour train in August, 1946. (Courtesy Jim Scribbins)

AN RS-3, NO. 487 enters Englewood with an outbound week day mid-afternoon train composed of one ex-C&NW and three regular Rock Island commuter coaches. These locomotives were the mainstay of Rock Island suburban power until the Fall of 1968. Many of the standard coaches have been replaced by the push pull equipment, and old cars remaining in service are now being painted a bright green. (Courtesy Jim Scribbins)

A FAIRBANKS-MORSE TYPE H-15-44 with Lowey styling leads an outbound rush hour train through Englewood. One of two such locomotives owned by the Rock Island, both were re-engined by EMD and retired with the advent of the new push pull trains. (Courtesy Jim Scribbins)

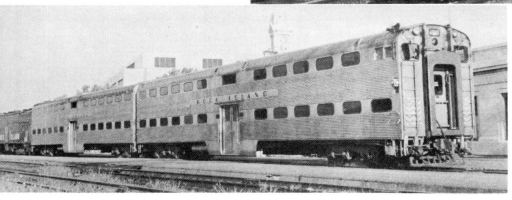

ROCK ISLAND ALCO RS-2, No. 489 waits patiently for its late evening departure time for a local run to Blue Island. (Courtesy Burdell Bulgrin, Rail Photo Service)

A ROCK ISLAND PUSH PULL TRAIN at Joliet, Illinois. Most non rush hour service consists of two car trains, such as this one. Double deck equipment is now used for nearly all non rush hour trains with the old standard equipment being used only during the rush hours. (Courtesy Bob Lorenz)

AFTER A SPECIAL TRIP TO LOS ANGELES on the Santa Fe, and Los Angeles—Las Vegas service on the Union Pacific and inter-city service on the NYC and PRR, both Aerotrains ended up as Rock Island suburban trains. Virtually G.M. busses on rail, in suburban service they had some of their cars coupled into the train backwards since equipment was not turned. This off peak train is departing Englewood for LaSalle Station in April, 1965. (Courtesy Jim Scribbins)

THE CAB B UNITS BUILT BY EMD and used on the Colorado Springs section of the Rocky Mountain Rocket have been rebuilt for push pull service. The two units have had their steam generators removed and diesel electric generators installed in their place. This rebuilding and a new modern paint scheme with a yellow nose have given the units a new lease on life—and they are still hauling passengers. The units originally had only one 1,000 HP engine and a baggage compartment. Now they have two 1,000 HP engines as the result of rebuilding in 1965. The units are custom built E-6's. (Courtesy Bob Lorenz)

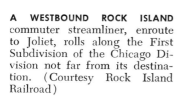

A WESTBOUND ROCK ISLAND commuter streamliner, enroute to Joliet, rolls along the First Subdivision of the Chicago Division not far from its destination. (Courtesy Rock Island Railroad)

The Illinois Central

The Illinois Central Railroad's commuter line serves the south part of Chicago and its southern suburbs. The suburban route consists of a separate electrified system between Randolph Street, Chicago and Richton, a distance of 29.33 miles; a branch line from 67th Street to 91st Street, both in Chicago, a distance of 3.94 miles; and a branch from Kensington to Blue Island, a distance of 3.31 miles. Over these three routes, the IC carries over 78,000 week day passengers and operates 267 week day trains. This traffic reduces to 205 trains on Saturday and 126 on Sunday. At the present time (1969), the IC operates more suburban trains than any other Chicago Railroad.

Not all the above trains operate from the Randolph Street Station. A few of the trains are operated as connection service on the branches or between 67th Street and Kensington. A breakdown of the trains operated shows 64 arrivals and departures at Blue Island, 107 at South Chicago and 78 at Richton. Non rush hour frequency varies from 20 minutes to one hour depending upon the time of day. Night time service is every two hours from 12:30 A.M. until 5:10 A.M. on the Richton and South Chicago lines. The Blue Island line's last train departs Chicago at 12:30 A.M. Off hour trains consist of 2 and 4 cars.

Rush hour service on the IC is quite a show. During the morning from 6 A.M. to 9 A.M., there are 41 IC and 8 South Shore Railroad arrivals at Randolph Street. During the evening from 4 P.M. to 6 P.M., there are 35 IC and 7 South Shore Railroad departures from Randolph. Most of these rush hour trains are made up of 8 and 10 car trains. One can watch this display of trains quite easily from the Jackson Boulevard overpass, east of Michigan Avenue.

IC suburban service has an impressive 97% on time record. The primary reason for this is that no thru passenger or freight trains occupy the electric line trackage.

The Illinois Central Suburban line, at the time of this writing, is undergoing a rather complete change. In fact, by the end of 1970, IC service will be well on its way to being completely modernized. Train schedules, ticketing arrangements and equipment are now either in the process of being changed or will be changed soon.

The present conversion involves the fare system. Two things are happening here. First, ticketing has been converted to an Automatic Revenue Collection System. The principle is quite simple. Ticket-activated gates are controlled by a small computer adjacent to gate areas to all stations. When a passenger inserts a ticket in a slot, the computer decodes the information on the back of the magnetic oxide-coated ticket. If the ticket is valid as to date, location, route and number of rides, the computer opens the gate and retains the ticket if it has been fully used or returns it if additional rides remain. This ticketing arrangement is one of the most advanced systems to be found anywhere in the world.

With this automatic ticket collection, there is no need to punch tickets on board the trains. Therefore, trains of 2 to 6 cars are handled by a conductor and an engineer. Trains of 8 to 10 cars have an additional crewman, a collector.

The IC is simplifying its fare structure by experimenting with a uniform fare on a zone basis. Under this plan, the suburban stations are grouped into five zones. Zone A includes the South Chicago Branch and all main line stations from Randolph Street to 95th Street. Zones B, C, D and E each include four main line stations. In addition, Zone C includes the Blue Island Branch.

At the present time, the IC provides train service with 274 standard electric MU coaches. These operate in married pairs of one motor and one trailer. The cars contain 84 seats each and were built in 1925-1926. The cars are not air conditioned and

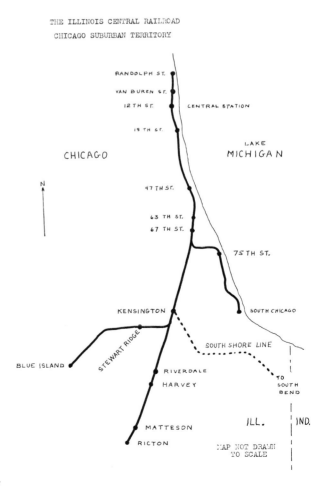

THE ILLINOIS CENTRAL RAILROAD
CHICAGO SUBURBAN TERRITORY

ALL ILLINOIS CENTRAL ELECTRIC COACHES operate in married pairs of one motor and one trailer as shown here with this mid-day local suburban train. (Courtesy Illinois Central)

contain no rest rooms. They are powered by 1,500 volt DC electricity received by car pantographs from an overhead wire.

After nearly 44 years of faithful service, the cars are soon to be replaced by 130 double deck electric MU coaches. It marks for the first time that equipment of this type will be electrified. The new cars will have 152 seats and entry and exit will be through the center. They will have tinted safety glass and air conditioning and a proposed top speed of 75 MPH. The new cars are expected to cost $38 million.

The purchase of the new equipment is being done through a plan with the Chicago South Suburban Mass Transit District. The IC will lease the cars from the District, but will maintain and repair the cars at its own expense. All the present cars will be scrapped upon delivery of the new cars. With the arrival of the new cars, schedules will be changed to fit the higher capacities of the trains.

Suburban railroad service does its best job hauling passengers along the city-suburb corridor, not within the city. Within the city service means competition with the local transit service. This is poor competition to say the least, and the IC is working toward co-ordinating service with the Chicago Transit Authority. An example of this planning includes a CTA-IC transfer plan, whereby the IC passenger can use the CTA to reach an IC commuter station, ride the train, and then transfer back to the CTA without having to pay another CTA fare. Another feature of CTA-IC co-operation is a joint study of various operations.

The Illinois Central is now also involved in a study which is developing a plan to improve the quality of service, schedules and equipment, develop optimal bus routes to coordinate with rail lines, extend present rail and bus service, and to consider the economic impact of the proposed changes. The study is being made by the Southward Transit Area Coordinating Committee, which is composed of public agencies, bus lines and commuter railroads in the south Suburban Chicago and Northern Indiana area.

The Illinois Central has been able to successfully weather some very tough times in the past few years. Although the commuter operation is now grossing approximately $9 million annually, in 1968, the suburban operation had a net profit of only $640,200. During the last 20 years, the IC suburban service has had a net income for only 9 of those years. The IC has worked very diligently to provide a fast, clean suburban service; now with new cars in prospect and its automatic revenue collection system in operation, the future of the Illinois Central suburan service has never been brighter.

MOST OF THE ILLINOIS CENTRAL RAILROAD suburban trackage in Chicago is elevated. However, on the two branch lines, most of trackage is on the surface or ground level. This four car non rush hour train is enroute to South Chicago on the South Shore District Branch Line. (The reader should not confuse this branch with the South Shore Railroad.) (Courtesy Bob Lorenz)

ALL ILLINOIS CENTRAL SUBURBAN STATIONS have high level platforms as shown here in this winter scene. (Courtesy Illinois Central)

BETWEEN RUSH HOURS, the Illinois Central services and stores its suburban equipment at the electric coach yard south of Central Station. (Courtesy Illinois Central)

A MODEL OF THE PROPOSED new Illinois Central double deck commuter car. As of early 1969, a final design had not yet been decided upon. (Courtesy Illinois Central)

THE ILLINOIS CENTRAL electric suburban service and main line service are actually two separate facilities. This is illustrated here with the electric line to the left and the main line to the right. In this photo, the Panama Limited, at 79 mph, has just passed a suburban train in the left background. (Courtesy Illinois Central)

THE NEW ILLINOIS CENTRAL Automatic Revenue Collection Gates at the Randolph Street Station in Chicago. (Courtesy Illinois Central)

Chicago South Shore and South Bend Railroad

The South Shore is the principle suburban service southeast and east of Chicago. The Railroad operates an electric Multiple-Unit passenger train service between Chicago, Gary, Michigan City and South Bend.

The South Shore is often referred to as the last interurban railroad operating in the United States. However, the South Shore does not look much like the usual picture of an interurban. In the first place, the passenger equipment is Class I Railroad size instead of the smaller interurban equipment. Secondly, the railroad operates long freight trains with high horsepower electric locomotives from General Electric. Third, the railroad operates over the Illinois Central from Kensington, Illinois to down town Chicago. Fourth, the CSS&SB is controlled by the Chesapeake and Ohio Railroad. In addition, the road has operated in a Class I manner and grosses $8 million annually, much more than the Class I minimum of $5 million for such classification. Unfortunately, the railroad is now in a financial predicament, having had a continuous passenger deficit since 1951. The freight service, as usual, has kept the road in the black until 1967, when the Company suffered a deficit of $18,107.

The South Shore operates an excellent suburban service between Chicago and South Bend. To maintain this service, the Road owns a total of 64 electric, multiple unit passenger cars. 12 of the cars are combination cars, while 14 are trailers. The balance of the equipment is made up of 60 foot and 78 foot electric coaches. These cars are used in trains ranging in length from one to eight cars, depending upon the time of the day.

The South Shore, at the time of this writing, is working toward a financial arrangement for the purchase of new passenger equipment. However, the plans are not yet finalized. The present equipment is becoming quite old (over 40 years of age), and it is becoming more and more difficult to obtain parts.

The CSS&SB operates 25 eastbound trains out of Chicago, and 24 westbound trains into Chicago on week days. On week-end, this number drops by about a third on Saturdays, and almost in half on Sundays. Of the 25 eastbound trains, only 19 operate beyond Gary to Michigan City. Of this, only 11 trains continue on to South Bend. Westbound, the exact reverse is true, except that there is one less train from Michigan City to Chicago, and consequently, one less train from Gary.

The mid day and evening service frequency is about every two hours to and from South Bend. From Michigan City, this service varies from one to two hours.

The rush hour service is, of course, much more frequent. During the morning rush hour, two trains originate from South Bend; four trains from Michigan City and two trains from Gary for a total of 8 trains arriving at Chicago. Three of these trains are scheduled only 5 minutes apart, and most of the trains are 15 minutes apart. The six trains originating east of Gary pick up additional cars at the Gary Station. The slowest local makes the 31 mile run from Gary to Chicago in 52 minutes, while the fastest express takes 45 minutes. This is very good time considering loading time at stations, that the trains are 6 to 8 cars long and are carrying up to 600 passengers. During the evening rush, there are seven trains dispatched from Chicago spaced approximately 15 minutes apart.

The CSS&SB owns 76 route miles of track and has trackage rights on an additional 14 miles on the Illinois Central between Kensington and Chicago. The Road serves 5 Illinois Central stations along the route: 63rd Street, 57th Street (Univ. of Chicago Campus), Central Station, Van Buren Street (Chicago Loop) and the final terminal, Randolph Street.

The Company services its passenger equipment at the Randolph Street Station in Chicago, Gary, Michigan City Shops and South Bend. These are the originating and terminating stations on the South Shore.

Looking back over the years, the Company was once quite prosperous. The automobile and the Indiana Toll Road and the Tri-State Expressway have dealt the Electric line staggering blows. At one point in its history, the South Shore borrowed Illinois Central MU equipment to accomodate week end traffic. But the automobile changed all of that.

Despite the drop in business and cut backs in service over the last ten years, the largest gap in train service out of Chicago is only 3½ hours—and that is from 2:30 A.M. to 6:00 A.M. At this time, the Company is carrying over 12,000 passengers on week days.

The new highways, however, are becoming self-defeating. It is becoming increasingly difficult to drive to Chicago, and even harder to park once you get there. Northwest Indiana is one of the fastest growing regions in the United States. This growth and traffic problem indicates that the South Shore will soon have a passenger traffic potential that will be the highest in their history, which, hopefully, will guarantee the survival and growth of what some people call "The Last Interurban."

ORIGINALLY, ALL SOUTH SHORE passenger equipment was 60 feet long. In fact, even the dining cars were 60 footers. During the 1940's and early 50's, the South Shore upgraded all passenger equipment, which resulted in the lengthening of several coaches and combination cars, such as the three car train shown here in street running in Michigan City, Indiana. Many of the cars lengthened to 78 feet were rebuilt with air conditioning and picture windows. The South Shore also owns two baggage cars for emergency package service. The Railroad carried U. S. Mail until 1968, when they lost their contract to trucks. (Courtesy Franklin A. King)

AN EARLY MORNING EASTBOUND South Shore passenger train has stopped at Hammond, Indiana to detrain passengers from Chicago. This particular train is enroute to Gary, and the two cars wil be added to a westbound rush hour train to Chicago after a quick inspection and the seats have been turned. (Courtesy Louis Dorin)

DURING A COLD SNAP in January, 1969, which put several South Shore passenger cars into the shops, 6 Illinois Central MU coaches were borrowed to aleviate the shortage of equipment. Yellow cards placed in the windows indicated that cars were actually in South Shore Line service. This same procedure was followed when the CSS&SB leased IC equipment during and after World War II. This photograph was taken at the Gary station after the evening rush. (Photo courtesy *Gary Post Tribune*)

WERE IT NOT FOR A BUSY freight service, the Chicago South Shore & South Bend Railroad would have gone the way of the old Chicago, North Shore and Milwaukee Line and the Chicago, Aurora & Elgin. The South Shore is the sole survivor of the Chicago Area triumverate and of the great midwestern interurban empire that once comprised nearly 9,000 miles. Neither the North Shore nor the CA&E had much of a freight service.

Today, South Shore freight service functions as a bridge line. Less than one third of the freight handled on the CSS&SB originates or terminates on the railroad. The line is also involved in Unit Coal train operations with pool cabooses with the Chicago & Eastern Illinois Railroad. Freight revenue amounts to around $4 million annually.

The South Shore owns three of these "Little Joes" for freight service along with several ex New York Central electrics and one diesel switcher. (Courtesy Burdell Bulgrin, Rail Photo Service)

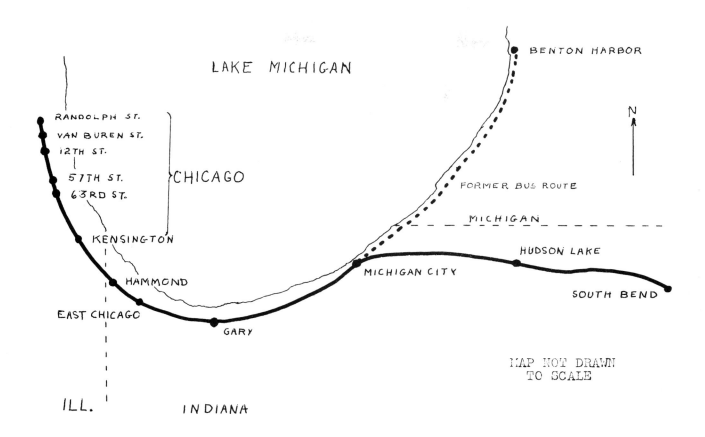

The Gulf, Mobile and Ohio Railroad

Although the GM&O is the only passenger hauler between Chicago and St. Louis, it has one of the smaller commuter operations out of Chicago. The railroad operates only one train in each direction between Chicago and Joliet, Illinois, a distance of 37.2 miles.

The GM&O operates from the Union Station to Joliet via Halsted Street (Chicago), Brighton Park, Glenn, Summit, Willow Springs, Lemont and Lockport. This route is completely different from the Rock Island, which also operates between Chicago and Joliet.

The GM&O operates a short but comfortable train. Its usual consist is 3 standard coaches with either an F-3 or an F-7 for power. The northbound run of No. 16 takes 1 hour and 5 minutes, while the southbound run of No. 17 takes only 50 minutes. The commuter district is double track and is protected by a modern signal system.

Even though the GM&O operates only two commuter trains on a daily except Saturday and Sunday basis, the commuter district service is not restricted to just those two trains. In addition, passengers southbound to Lemont and Lockport may ride No. 5, the Midnight Special, a late evening train from Chicago to St. Louis. Joliet passengers proper may also ride No. 1, The Limited, a noontime train, and No. 3, the Abraham Lincoln, a late afternoon train, on the week ends. Northbound in the commuter area Joliet passengers proper may also ride the Midnight Special which arrives Chicago in the early morning. All equipment operated on GM&O trains, both commuter and through, is Air Conditioned and kept in immaculate condition by the Gulf, Mobile and Ohio Railroad.

THE GM&O'S STREAMLINER, "The Abraham Lincoln," is shown here departing the Chicago Union Station. This train serves local Joliet passengers on week ends only, when the suburban train does not operate. (Courtesy Gulf, Mobile & Ohio Railroad)

MOTIVE POWER ON THE GM&O'S short commuter train is generally an E.M.D. 1500 Horsepower F-3 equipped with a steam generator. These locomotives provide adequate power for the three car trains, and often are MU'd with E units on the long distance passenger trains. (Courtesy Electro-Motive Division)

THE GM&O OPERATES streamlined equipment on through trains that handle passengers between Chicago and Joliet. (Courtesy Gulf, Mobile & Ohio Railroad)

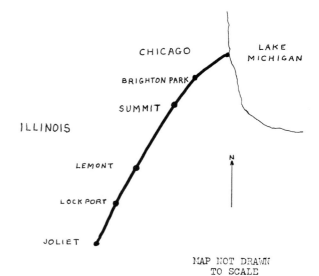

THE GULF, MOBILE AND OHIO RAILROAD
CHICAGO SUBURBAN TERRITORY

CHICAGO
LAKE MICHIGAN
BRIGHTON PARK
SUMMIT
ILLINOIS
LEMONT
LOCKPORT
JOLIET

N

MAP NOT DRAWN
TO SCALE

The Norfolk and Western Railway

The Norfolk and Western (formerly the Wabash) is another one of the small Chicagoland commuter operations. The N&W's commuter district extends from Chicago's Dearborn Station to Orland Park, a distance of 23.2 miles. This is one of the shortest districts in the Chicago area.

The N&W operates one train in each direction on a daily except Saturday and Sunday basis. The usual consist for this train is five air conditioned coaches with a GP-7 for power. The northbound train, No. 112, leaves Orland Park at 6:55 A.M. and arrives at Chicago at 8:00 A.M. The Southbound train, No. 113, departs Chicago at 5:30 P.M. and arrives in Orland Park at 6:22 P.M.

This particular commuter train has a little more history to it then the average train in this type of service. At one point in its history, the train operated between Chicago and Decatur, Illinois, a distance of 172.5 miles. The train performed commutation service for the Chicago suburbs, therefore it had to leave Decatur around 1:30 A.M. in order to reach Chicago at 8:00 A.M. This northbound schedule was convenient for the mail and express traffic that it carried over ten years ago. The southbound schedule was much more convenient for passengers. It left Chicago around 5:40 P.M. and arrived in Decatur at 9:27 P.M.

Although the N&W operation is very small, it does provide the only all-weather transportation service to several Southwestern Chicago suburbs.

IN ADDITION TO THE CHICAGO-DECATUR TRAIN, the former Wabash once operated this daily commuter between Chicago and Landers, Illinois, the sight of a present day Norfolk and Western classification yard. Steamer No. 659 is a 4-4-0 and it handled a single combine for the run. (Courtesy H. W. Pontin, Rail Photo Service)

THE FORMER WABASH RAILROAD operated various types of Pacific steam locomotives on their Chicago-Decatur local, such as the No. 675. Steam power was replaced by GP-9's on this commuter run. (Courtesy Norfolk and Western Ry.)

THE NORFOLK & WESTERN RAILWAY uses five former thru train coaches in their Chicago Suburban run. These coaches, such as the No. 1234, have a seating capacity of 68 passengers and all are air conditioned. (Courtesy Jim Scribbins)

AN INTERIOR VIEW of Wabash coach No. 1234. The new luggage racks and bullet lights and dropped ceiling indicate extensive rebuilding just after World War II. Upon assignment to the suburban run, the reclining seats were replaced by non recliners fixed face to face in pairs since the equipment is never wyed. (Courtesy Jim Scribbins)

PENNSY K-4'S ALSO DID THE HONORS on the Chicago Valparaiso commuter runs. Here an unusual double header on the Valpo bound rush hour run races neck and neck with a Burlington Zephyr by 22nd Street, Chicago in 1949. This shot was a close call for the lensman, as he had to lay flat between the trains after he had clicked the shutter. (Courtesy J. R. Crosby, Rail Photo Service)

The Penn Central Company

The Penn Central operates a commuter service between Chicago and Valparaiso, Indiana, a distance of 43.6 miles. The Company operates two commuter trains in each direction Monday through Friday. The trains operate during the morning and evening rush hours. The first train leaves Valparaiso at 5:55 A.M. and takes one hour and 10 minutes for the run to Chicago. This train consists of two cars and a GP-9 and operates for the early workers in Chicago and the 7 A.M. shift employees at the steel mills and oil refineries in the Whiting-Indiana Harbor Area. The second train, which makes all stops, leaves Valparaiso at 6:35 A.M. and takes one hour and 15 minutes for the inbound trip. This train consists of a GP-9 and four coaches. Naturally, this train carries the majority of the commuters.

In the evening, the reverse operation takes place. The first train leaves the Chicago Union Station at 5:05 P.M. and makes all stops to Valparaiso. This train consists of four coaches. Its running time is 75 minutes. The second train leaves at 5:40 P.M. and takes 65 minutes for the outbound run.

The Penn Central's suburban service is not, however, limited to the two commuter trains. Additional trains (to and from New York), such as No. 23, 55 and 53 also stop at Valparaiso and Gary on their west bound runs. Eastbound, No. 22, 48, 50 and 54 stop at Gary and Valparaiso. These trains provide noon, afternoon and evening service for anyone traveling between Chicago and the above points. Therefore, the public has a choice of five inbound and six outbound trains. These trains and the commutation trains provide a convenient service for about 375 daily passengers that live near the Penn Central Main Line between Chicago and Valparaiso.

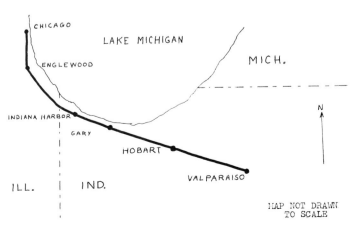

THE PENN CENTRAL COMPANY
CHICAGO SUBURBAN TERRITORY

153

PRIOR TO THE MID-1960'S, the former New York Central operated a suburban service from Chicago to Elkhart, Indiana. Before discontinuance, the service consisted of one inbound rush hour train and two outbound during the morning and evening respectively. Up until the early and mid 1950's, however, the road operated quite an extensive service between Chicago and Porter, Chesterton and La Porte, Indiana. The NYC line paralleled the Pennsy all the way to Gary, and it also paralleled the South Shore much of this distance. The New York Central operated type K-3n Pacifics with rebuilt tenders to permit back up running on these locals. The consist of the trains always included a combination car. After dieselization, motive power consisted of either E units or Geeps. The 4856 is arriving at Englewood with a local from Porter, Indiana. (Courtesy Harold E. Williams, Rail Photo Service)

IN ADDITION to providing commuter train service to Gary and Valparaiso from Chicago, four Penn Central thru trains in each direction stop at those two points. One of those trains is No. 48, the old "General", shown here departing the Chicago Union Station in early 1950's. Today, No. 48 is still running and providing early rush hour commuters a ride home. In addition, the train is minus the many head end cars, the Fairbanks-Morse power and has a different name, "The Broadway Limited" since No. 28 and 29 have been discontinued. Another difference is that the "Empire Builder" no longer arrives at Chicago during the departure of No. 48 as the latter has a later departure time. (Courtesy Bob Lorenz)

STANDARD OPERATING PROCEDURE on the Valpo commuter trains today (1969) is one GP-9 equipped with a steam generator. On rare occasions, when there is a special party originating and terminating within the suburban territory—such as a school party going to Chicago—two units will be used. The single units provide ample power for the two and four car trains that make up the usual consist of the Valpo Locals. (Courtesy Penn Central)

Chapter 7
SAN FRANCISCO

The Southern Pacific Company

The Southern Pacific Company operates a suburban service between San Francisco and San Jose, a distance of 46.9 miles. The SP carries approximately 11,000 passengers each day, Monday through Friday on 44 week day trains. This number reduces to 24 on Saturdays and to 18 on Sundays.

As with other suburban roads, the SP operates over half of their week day service during the rush hours. During the 6 A.M. to 9 A.M. period, there are 12 arrivals at the SP's Third Street Terminal. From 4 P.M. to 7 P.M., there are 10 departures. The frequency of rush hour service varies from 3 minutes to 19 minutes between trains. Non rush hour service frequency varies from 55 minutes to 2 hours, 35 minutes. Week day service begins at 5:05 A.M. and runs until 12:35 A.M. All trains, except one rush hour train, arrive and depart from San Jose.

The SP uses a Zone Fare System. The suburban territory is divided into 6 zones, with each zone covering three or four stations between South San Francisco and San Jose. A passenger may ride to or from any station within the zone for which his ticket is good.

In order to handle the present volume of traffic, the SP maintains 55 standard coaches and 46 double deck streamlined coaches. The last group of 15 double deck cars was delivered early in 1969. These cars have a seating capacity of 160 passengers and are air conditioned. All non rush hour trains are equipped with the streamlined double deck cars.

Motive power used on the Peninsula Commuter service varies from GP-9's and Fairbanks-Morse 2400 HP Roadswitchers to EMD F-7's and E-8's. These locomotives come from a motive power pool and are equipped with steam generators. SP suburban trains are operated in the conventional manner.

The Southern Pacific operates the only suburban service west of Chicago. San Francisco is a very beautiful city and it is surrounded on three sides by water. The city, like others in the east, is suffering from highway traffic strangulation. To build new highways into Frisco has been recognized by civic leaders to be self defeating. The city cannot expand its boundries. To build new expressways and parking ramps would actually destroy the down town area. The SP is quite capable of handling many more passengers to and from suburbia. Automobile traffic is continuing to increase. This situation should produce thought waves that there must be a better way to travel down town. Since the SP already has a fine suburban service, the result should mean an increase in both rush hour and non rush hour traffic. This in turn should improve the financial situation for the Southern Pacific's Suburban Operations.

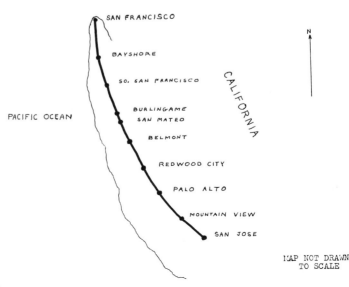

THE SOUTHERN PACIFIC COMPANY
SAN FRANCISCO SUBURBAN TERRITORY

MAP NOT DRAWN TO SCALE

DURING THE DAYS OF STEAM, the SP operated a variety of power including 4-6-0's, 4-6-2's and 4-8-2's. This photo shows an evening suburban local to San Jose behind a 4-6-0 oil burner in 1934. Note the RPO-Baggage behind the steamer. Several commuter trains throughout the United States and Canada carried Mail and Express until after the Second World War, and some even carried mail until 1968. This occurred on the SP when the LA-Frisco mail train terminated at San Jose, and the mail cars and RPO were handled on two of the commuter runs. (Courtesy G. M. Best, Rail Photo Service)

TO THIS WRITER'S KNOWLEDGE, the last suburban train in the United States to carry a RPO car was SP train No. 145. This train forwarded the RPO to San Francisco from San Jose, the northern terminal for a Los Angeles Mail Train. This operation was discontinued on February 4, 1966.

THE SOUTHERN PACIFIC assigns Fairbanks-Morse 2400 HP Roadswitchers to most of its suburban trains. Here the 3021 is backing to the San Francisco depot to work commuter train No. 140.

RUSH HOUR, NORTHBOUND NO. 123 arriving at San Francisco at 8:00 A.M., right on schedule.

NORTHBOUND TRAIN NO. 173 enroute to San Francisco arriving at Santa Clara, California. 173 is a mid afternoon, Saturday only schedule. The consist of the train is the usual off hour accommodations, two double deck suburban coaches.

AN EVENING PORTRAIT of rush hour trains awaiting departure from the San Francisco station. From left to right are trains No. 130, 132, 136, 134, and 138. Beginning at 5:14 these trains will depart the stub end depot on three minute headways.

SOUTHBOUND RUSH HOUR TRAIN No. 136 departs San Francisco at 5:23 P.M. and runs non stop to Burlingame, a distance of 16.3 miles. From that point to San Jose, the train retains its "Express" status by stopping at only 7 of the 15 stations between Burlingame to San Jose. Of the 11 trains departing San Francisco between 4:00 P.M. and 6:00 P.M., only three of the trains are locals. All others are expresses but schedules are set up so that most stations in the 46.9 mile suburban territory are served by at least two south bound rush hour runs during the time period. This means that nearly all commuters can have a faster ride home than could otherwise be provided if all trains operated as locals.

NORTH OF SAN JOSE, trains 126 and 141, the "Del Monte" carries suburban equipment. The extra cars are added or detached at San Jose depending upon direction. Southbound, the "Del Monte" serves as a rush hour train to San Jose. At that point, the train will lose all but three cars before it continues its southbound run. Northbound, the train serves as a mid-morning suburban run within the commuter territory. No. 126 is shown here near Paul Avenue in San Francisco.

SOUTH OF SAN JOSE, the "Del Monte" is a very short train and has been for many years. The train operates between San Francisco and Pacific Grove, a distance of about 120 miles. The train's equipment includes reclining seat chair cars and a Parlor Snack Lounge car. This photo shows the "Del Monte" running as train No. 139 near Lapiz Siding in April, 1962.

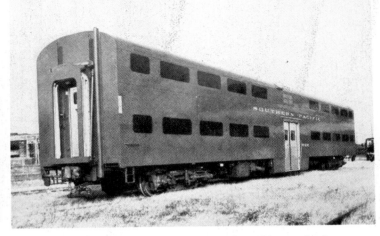

THE NORTHBOUND "DEL MONTE" picks up additional suburban equipment during its stop at San Jose. Here No. 141 is arriving at San Francisco with the usual three car consist from Monterey plus two double deck suburban coaches.

SOUTHERN PACIFIC SUBURBAN COACH No 3745 was the last car constructed of a 15 car order placed with Pullman in 1968. The total cost of the new equipment, which provides more than 2400 seats, was in excess of $3 million. The new equipment is quite similar to the 31 double deck coaches the SP has had in service since 1955. The exterior of the new coaches is painted SP grey with white lettering (Courtesy Pullman Standard)

A SOUTHERN PACIFIC morning rush hour commuter train approaching San Francisco with a mixed consist of both streamlined and standard suburban coaches. Note the crowded free way parallel to the SP's main line. As the rush hour continues the traffic will become even more congested. (Courtesy Southern Pacific Company)

ONE MIGHT THINK that ticket collection on the double deck cars would be a slow process because of the two levels of passengers. In this photo, the conductor is punching a young lady's ticket on the lower level. Right above the conductor's cap is the upper level floor. Passengers on that level can easily place their tickets in clips on the edge of the balcony while sitting in their seats. The conductor only has to reach up to eye level for upper deck tickets. There is no wasted motion at all. (Courtesy Southern Pacific Company)

THE DOORS ON THE DOUBLE DECK suburban coaches are designed for the loading or unloading of three passengers at a time. This means that although the capacity of the coaches is over 150 passengers, loading and unloading can be done quite rapidly. (Courtesy Southern Pacific)

AN INTERIOR VIEW of the lower or main floor of the new Southern Pacific suburban coaches. All seats on this level are designed for two passengers. (Courtesy Pullman Standard)

AS THE READER CAN SEE, there are two types of seating arrangements on the upper decks of the two level suburban coaches. The parcel rack shown in the lower right of the photo is for main floor passengers. All seats, except the wall type theatre seats, are reversible through a flip over design. (Courtesy Pullman Standard)

AN INTERIOR VIEW of the upper deck coaches recently placed into service by the Southern Pacific. Note the baggage and parcel rack for upper deck passengers in the left center of the photo. (Courtesy Pullman Standard)

PRIOR TO THE DELIVERY of SDP-35's and SDP-45's, the "Coast Daylight" was handled by two unit FP-7's. No. 99 is shown here at Salinas, California with two such units and a six car train in May, 1967.

TODAY (1969) THE "COAST DAYLIGHT" is the only through train operating through the Suburban Territory. Number 99 and 98 stop only at Palo Alto and San Jose and Twenty Ride Family, one way and round trip tickets are honored within the Suburban Territory. Commutation tickets, however, are not honored on these two trains.

The reader will notice the SDP-45, No. 3208 is not carrying train numbers. Train numbers were discontinued on through trains in 1967. Today, only the suburban passenger trains continue to carry train identification numbers. This photo shows No. 98 at Salinas, California, about 90 minutes south of the suburban territory.

BEFORE ITS DISCONTINUANCE IN 1968, the Southern Pacific's "Lark" played a part in the Peninsula Suburban service. On the Southbound trip, No. 76 departed San Francisco around 9:00 P.M. and stopped at Burlingame, Palo Alto and San Jose. On the Northbound trip from Los Angeles No. 75 made the same stops between San Jose and San Francisco, and arrived at the Third Street Terminal during the morning rush at 8:30 A.M. This photo shows the "Lark" arriving at San Francisco on a Sunday morning in 1966, 10 minutes ahead of time. Only regular one way and round trip tickets were honored on the "Lark" within the commutation territory.

Chapter 8

MONTREAL, TORONTO AND DETROIT

The Canadian Pacific Railway

The Canadian Pacific operates a suburban service over three lines out of Montreal, Quebec. The largest suburban operation is the Montreal-Rigaud line, a distance of 40.2 miles. The other two territories are the Montreal-Ste-Therese line, a distance of 25.6 miles; and the Montreal-Farnham line, a distance of 43.2 miles. Altogether, these three lines carry an average of 16,000 week day passengers.

The Montreal-Rigaud service is the major CP suburban train operation in the Montreal area. At this time, there are 12 trains operated in each direction on week days. This reduces to 4 and 3 on Saturdays and Sundays respectively. Most of the train operation is during the morning and evening rush hours. From 7:30 A.M. until 9:00 A.M., there are 7 arrivals at the Montreal Windsor Station. There are 8 departures from Montreal during the 4:00 P.M.-6:00 P.M. period. Therefore, over 60% of the trains operated on this line are rush hour trains.

The majority of the trains operate to and from Rigaud. However, many of the rush hour trains operate to and from Vaudreuil, which is 23.7 miles from Montreal. Suburban trains are serviced at Montreal during layover, and are stored overnight at both Rigaud and Vaudreuil.

In addition to the 12 week day trains, two daily Montreal Ottawa trains in each direction make certain stops in the suburban territory. These are the Streamliner "Rideau," trains 233 and 234; and trains 232 and 235. The "Canadian," trains 1 and 2 also make some stops in the suburban territory, but do not carry passengers locally within the territory.

All week end service and 10 of the 24 week day trains are equipped with Rail Diesel Cars. The RDC equipment for the suburban trains is drawn from the Montreal RDC pool. Other trains are equipped with both streamlined and standard suburban coaches. Most of the standard cars, are now being replaced by 9 double deck stainless steel push pull coaches. These cars are nearly identical to the equipment used on the Milwaukee Road in Chicago.

The line to Ste-Therese has only one rush hour train in each direction. This is a daily except Saturday and Sunday operation equipped with RDC's.

However, this service is supplemented by a morning and an evening train in each direction, for a total of four additional trains. These trains are RDC Dayliners and operate to and from Ottawa via Montebello. Saturday and Sunday service amounts to 3 and 2 trains, respectively, in each direction. These are through Montreal-Ottawa trains and they make certain stops in the suburban territory.

The only suburban territory that operates east of Montreal is the line to Farnham. Again there is only a single rush hour train, operated to Montreal in the morning, and to Farnham in the evening. These trains operate daily except Saturday and Sunday. Eastbound service is supplemented by a Daily late afternoon through Dayliner to Megantic, and the mid-evening departure of the Domeliner "Atlantic Limited." These two east bound trains make a few stops within the Suburban territory. Westbound, the "Atlantic Limited" arrives at Montreal during the rush hour and makes four stops within the suburban territory. The RDC Dayliner from Megantic departs Farnham about noon and makes six stops between Farnham and Montreal. This service provides some suburbanites with a choice of 3 trains in each direction. Week end service is provided by through trains making certain stops within the suburban territory. Saturday service consists of two trains in each direction. An additional train is operated on Sunday for a total of 3 trains in each direction.

The Canadian Pacific's suburban train operations are quite modern with the RDC's, stainless steel push pull equipment and the streamlined commuter cars. The CP has an up to date physical plant and will be able to handle efficiently the increases in traffic that are expected because of the increasing highway traffic problems in the Montreal Area.

A WESTBOUND CANADIAN PACIFIC commuter train on the Montreal Lake Shore Division with a DL-701 diesel unit and 5 cars. Three of the coaches are the 800 series. Note the baggage car on the head end, and the train is slowing for the station at Brucy. (Courtesy G. C. Corey, Rail Photo Service)

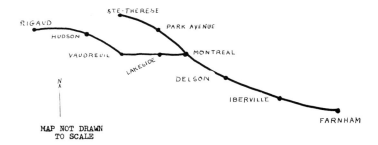

CANADIAN PACIFIC RAILWAY

MONTREAL SUBURBAN TERRITORY

STE-THERESE

RIGAUD   PARK AVENUE

HUDSON

VAUDREUIL   MONTREAL

LAKESIDE

N   DELSON

IBERVILLE

FARNHAM

MAP NOT DRAWN
TO SCALE

THE CANADIAN PACIFIC operates 40 of these 800 series coaches in suburban service. The cars have an exterior length of 83 feet, 11 inches and are steam heated. (Courtesy Canadian Pacific Railway)

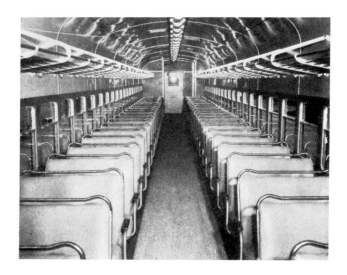

AN INTERIOR VIEW of the Canadian Pacific 800 series suburban coaches. These cars have an inside length of 74 feet, 3 inches and have a seating capacity of 103 passengers. The seats are reversible and luggage racks extend the entire length of the car on both sides. (Courtesy Canadian Pacific Railway)

THE CANADIAN PACIFIC first purchased Rail Diesel Cars in 1953. When the new cars arrived on the property, the CPR proudly displayed them both within the suburban territory of Montreal and around the Dominion. The Canadian Pacific owns a total of 54 RDC's and has nick-named them "Dayliners." While the majority of the cars are used in Montreal suburban service, many others are assigned to long distance runs out of Toronto, Halifax, Sudbury, Calgary, and Victoria. The Company presently owns 24 RDC-1's, 22 RDC-2's, 5 RDC-3's and 3 RDC-4's. All types but the "4's" are operated in the Montreal Pool. (Courtesy Canadian Pacific)

THE CANADIAN PACIFIC operates RDC-3's in through trains between Montreal and Ottawa and other points. RDC-3's are not normally assigned to suburban runs, but many commuters ride them when they use thru trains between the suburbs and Montreal. (Courtesy The Budd Co.)

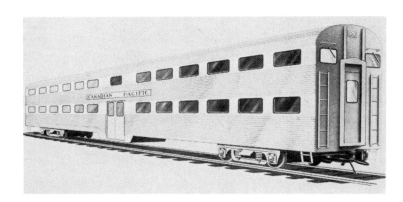

THE CANADIAN PACIFIC has placed a $2.8 million order with Canadian Vickers, Ltd. for nine double deck passenger cars which it plans to put into service on the Montreal suburban Lakeshore commuter run in June, 1969. The CPR is the first Canadian road to order push pull equipment which has been used successfully by several US roads. The order includes seven trailer cars each with a seating capacity of 168 and two cab control cars each with a capacity of 156. There is three abreast loading and unloading through sliding doors located at the center of the coach and are operated automatically from push botton control boxes. An electric element keeps the bottom step free of ice and snow in the winter. The cars are 85 feet long and their rail to rooftop height is 15 feet, 11 inches. By comparison, present lightweight cars are 13 feet, six inches from rail to rooftop. (Courtesy Canadian Pacific Railway)

EACH OF THE NEW DOUBLE DECK CARS has its own diesel operated power plant. In addition to air-conditioning, each has fluorescent lighting, attractive plastic-finished interiors, rubber filled cushion seats with flip over backs, and double glazed windows with an inside pane of graduated tinted safety glass. The lower level has two abreast seating on each side of the center aisle. The upper level consists of two balconies with single seating and an aisle on each side. Upper level seating consists of both regular seats and rows of wall-type, self-raising theatre seats. As on US double deck coaches, the conductor does his ticket collecting from the lower level only. Passengers in the balconies put their tickets on clips on panels running along the outer edge of each upper aisle. The conductors replace the tickets in the clips after they have been punched.

Parcel racks are provided on both levels. The engineman's cab is on the upper level and at one end of each control car. Washroom facilities are located in the control cars. (Courtesy Canadian Pacific Railway)

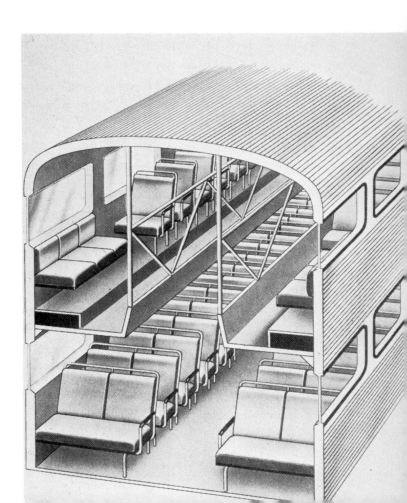

Canadian National

The Canadian National operates a suburban service over two lines and a branch line in the Montreal, Quebec area. The more important of the two main lines is the route to Deux-Montagnes, which includes a short branch from Val Royal to Cartierville. Deux-Montagnes is located 29.2 miles north of Montreal. Cartierville is 8.2 miles from the Montreal Depot. This suburban service is the only electrified passenger train operation in Canada.

The other suburban service runs east of Montreal to St. Hilaire, a distance of 20.7 miles.

On these two lines, the Canadian National carries nearly 49,000 week day passengers.

In order to provide service for these passengers, the CN operates 40 trains in each direction on the Deux-Montagnes line. However, only 21 of these trains operate in each direction from and to that point. Of these, 4 outbound and 3 inbound trains carry cars to and from Cartierville. A total of 19 trains in each direction operate between Montreal and Cartierville. During the morning and evening rush hours, there are 10 arrivals and 10 departures respectively at Montreal. These trains operate 10 to 20 minutes apart. Off hour service during the day is half hourly to Val Royal, with every other train operating to the two different suburban terminals. This service lengthens out to hourly after the evening rush. There are a total of 28 trains operated in each direction on Saturday, with 17 of these in each direction on the Deux-Montagnes line. Sunday service consists of 16 trains in each direction with 11 to and from Deux-Montagnes. Average running time between Montreal and Cartierville is 20 minutes, to Deux-Montagnes, 45 minutes.

On the St. Hilaire line, there is but one train inbound and one outbound to and from Montreal during the morning and evening rush hours. However, during the rush hours, a through train equipped with Rail Diesel Cars stops at two of the suburbs on this line during the week; and makes all stops on Saturdays when the commuter train does not run. There is no Sunday service.

In order to provide commuter service, the CNR maintains 6 Electric MU standard coaches with 11 trailers, and 30 standard coaches. The standard coaches are handled in the electrified territory by electric locomotives. The CNR owns nine such locomotives for this service. Otherwise, suburban trains are powered by diesel road switchers built by General Motors and Montreal Locomotive Works.

The Canadian National suburban service provides a convenient, all weather transportation system for thousands of Montreal suburbanites. With highway traffic being what it is, the CN's suburban service should have a very bright future.

CANADIAN NATIONAL
MONTREAL SUBURBAN TERRITORY

DEUX-MONTAGNES
LAVAL LINKS
CARTIERVILLE
VAL ROYAL
MONTREAL   OTTERBURN PARK   ST. HILAIRE

N

MAP NOT DRAWN
TO SCALE

A REAR VIEW of a Canadian National Class X-10 Suburban Type steam locomotive. The construction of these locomotives was ideal for reverse running. Notice the coal bunker and rear windows on the cab. The rear end was also equipped with a pilot and a strong headlight. (Courtesy Bob Lorenz)

TRAIN NO. 247, Vaudreuil commuter train, departing Central Station, Montreal behind tank steamer No. 46. The maximum speed for these X-10 class locomotives was 65 miles per hour. This photo was taken in 1953. (Courtesy S. K. Bolton, Jr., Rail Photo Service)

A NUMBER OF CANADIAN NATIONAL suburban trains were powered by Fairbanks Morse diesel units. Here the 7616 is shown with train No. 705 after crossing the Victoria Bridge over the St. Lawrence River. This photo was taken during the days when one could view steam, electric and diesel power at the same time on CNR suburban trains—1953. (Courtesy S. K. Bolton Jr., Rail Photo Service)

AN ELECTRICALLY POWERED RUSH HOUR commuter train, en route to Montreal, approaches the Mount Royal station with 12 4900 series coaches. The seating capacity of this train is well over 1100 passengers, and it will have many standees upon arrival at Montreal. (Courtesy Canadian National Railways)

CANADIAN NATIONAL MU ELECTRIC TRAINS are generally operated with one motor car and two trailers. However, all trailers are equipped with headlights and train controls so that two car trains are possible, that is, one motor and one trailer. The Canadian National electric service is the only such operation in Canada. (Courtesy Canadian National)

NON RUSH HOUR ELECTRIC TRAIN departing the Portal Heights Station at the North Entrance to the Mount Royal Tunnel at Montreal. (Courtesy Canadian National Railways)

AN OUTBOUND CNR electric train arriving at the Portal Heights station. (Courtesy Canadian National Railways)

AN EXTERIOR PORTRAIT of the 4900 series standard suburban coach operated by the Canadian National. The Road operates a total of 47 of these coaches, primarily in rush hour week day service. (Courtesy Canadian National Railways)

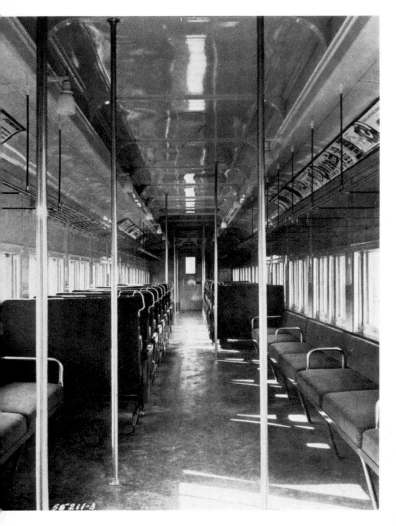

THE 4900 SERIES Canadian National suburban coaches have an interior more like rapid transit equipment than that of standard commuter cars. In this case, piping and poles are provided for standees and notice the side seating. Luggage racks are provided over the standard seats. These cars have a seating capacity of 92 to 95 passengers and have an inside length of 78 feet 1 inch. This equipment is steam heated. (Courtesy Canadian National Railways)

THE CANADIAN NATIONAL owns 8 RDC-3's. These cars are not generally operated in suburban service, except when they are part of a long distance train that stops within the suburban territory, such as on the line to St. Hyacinthe. (Courtesy the Budd Company)

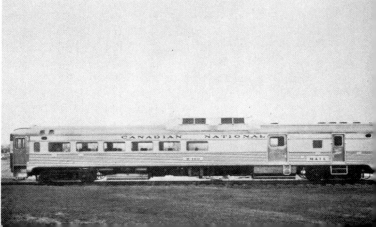

THE CANADIAN NATIONAL RDC's are also being painted in the new paint scheme. The scheme includes a blue band along the windows and the red front. The CNR owns 19 RDC-1's, many of which have been equipped with a snack bar. All RDC's are equipped with reclining seats. (Courtesy Canadian National Railways)

THE CANADIAN NATIONAL is always alert to any way in which idle equipment may be put to use. The RDC's are quite useful for special parties, etc. and then are operated as special trains, such as this passenger extra which is on a week end excursion.

The middle car of this particular train is a former Boston and Maine RDC-9. These cars have no operating controls and must be operated between two other RDC's. The Canadian National calls their RDC-9's RDC-5's. (Courtesy Canadian National Railways)

THE CANADIAN NATIONAL operates several RDC cars in Montreal suburban service, however the equipment is not restricted to that type of operation. This RDC-3 is in thru train service and has stopped for a publicity photo near Cambellton, New Brunswick. (Courtesy Canadian National)

Government of Ontario Transit

The Government of Ontario Transit, GO Transit for short, is a prime example of how railroad suburban service can improve public transportation. GO is operated by the Canadian National and it serves the eastern and western suburbs of Toronto. It is the newest passenger service in North America. The new service went into operation in May, 1967 and is now carrying well over 16,000 passengers every week day. The service is operated between Pickering and Hamilton, Ontario with Toronto Union Station located almost in the middle of the 60.2 mile long suburban territory.

GO's train operations exceed many other suburban operations. The service requires 52 week day trains to provide hourly service from 6:00 A.M. until mid-night and 20 minute headways during the rush hours. This reduces to 38 trains for hourly service on week ends and holidays. The bulk of the service operates between Oakville and Pickering. On week days, only four trains provide service to and from Hamilton.

Train length varies from two cars to ten cars depending upon the time of day. The service uses 54 coaches (Built by Hawker Siddeley), 8 of which are equipped with control cabs for push pull operation. The motive power for the push pull trains is elongated (by seven feet) GP/40's built by General Motors. The extra seven feet provides space for a diesel/alternator that supplies power for train heating or cooling and lighting. The Geeps are geared for 83 MPH. In addition, Hawker Siddeley built nine self propelled cars, similar to RDC's, that are used as two car scoots during off peak hours; and also to supplement the conventional trains during the rush hours.

The trains are serviced and cleaned at the Canadian National's Willowbrook Maintenance facility. The coach yard is near the Mimco Station. The trains are parked without uncoupling at Willowbrook. Fueling facilities are located on the train storage tracks so that the Geeps are uncoupled only if repairs are required. This is another cost saving feature so necessary in today's suburban operations.

Fares were developed for the purpose of being competitive with driving costs, including parking. This is the only way to get the motorist out of his car and on to the train. The result has been spectacular and the patronage has surpassed the forecasted traffic. The present annual deficit is around $2 million. A low price to pay compared with new highway construction.

GO Transit was established as an experimental project to weigh its efficiency against the highway mode of travel.

At this time, the continuing flow of data from this experiment are still being evaluated. Ontario authorities, however, believe that a modern transportation system must have an appropriately balanced combination of highways and public transit. Since this philosophy applies to every large city, this writer believes that the railroads will probably have an increasing role to play in the total transportation picture.

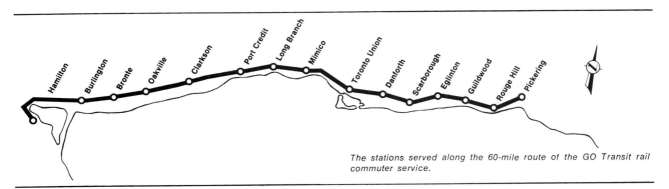

The stations served along the 60-mile route of the GO Transit rail commuter service.

THE GOVERNMENT OF ONTARIO TRANSIT operates locomotive model GP40TC's in its suburban service. The letters "TC" indicate that the locomotive is different from other GP40's and stand for Toronto Commuter. The length of these locomotives is 65'-7", which is one inch shorter than the SD 40. The maximum operating speed for these Geeps is 83 miles per hour. The locomotive will accelerate 10 coaches from 0 to 60 MPH, over most sections of the operation, in about 2½ minutes. A generator driven by a 12 cylinder 149 series Detroit Diesel engine will furnish 430 KW continuous, 470 KW intermittent of electrical power to provide controlled electrical heating, air conditioning and lighting in the coaches. This set is located behind the main engine. In the locomotive cab, as in each control cab in some of the coaches, there is a radio telephone and an intercom system. This enables the engineman to communicate with wayside personnel with the conductor or with the passengers. (Courtesy General Motors of Canada Ltd.)

GO PUSH PULL TRAIN departing the Toronto Union Station with the Toronto Skyline in the background. The GO self propelled cars are identical to the exteriors of the push pull cars, except for two small exhaust stacks. The paint scheme is brushed aluminum with white ends and a green GO symbol. Eleven large windows are placed along each side. The double width folding doors at both ends of each car may be electrically operated from any point in the train.

The coaches are carried on four wheel inboard bearing trucks. A steel coil and air spring assembly cushions the ride and provides that floor height remains constant regardless of the number of passengers. (Courtesy Ontario Department of Highways)

THE INTERIORS of the new GO push pull equipment is among the finest in North America. A considerable amount of time and effort was spent in designing the interior of the cars as styling and comfort play a very important part in luring the motorist away from his automobile. The predominant wall color is beige-gray with green on the bulkheads and rosewood and ebony on the center compartment walls. Floors are covered with a highly attractive and easily maintained seamless terrazzo like vinyl plastic. Ceilings of white translucent plastic panels are illuminated by fluorescent lights to highlight the bright interior appearance and provide glare-free night illumination. There are two passenger compartments, one seating 40 and the other 54. The bucket type seats (non-rotating) are grouped in facing pairs to achieve a sense of roominess while retaining a high seating capacity and ease of maintenance. Seating variety is provided by wall mounted seat groups at three locations in each car. (Courtesy Ontario Department of Highways)

THE CANADIAN NATIONAL MAIN LINE was rebuilt and additional track was laid to accommodate the new frequent GO Transit trains. Following is an example of track utilization and the use of CTC to minimize delays. (Courtesy GO Transit, "A New Approach To Urban Transportation" Page 29, Department of Highways, Ontario

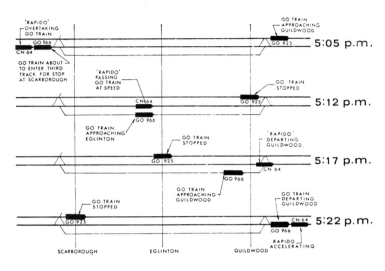

TYPICAL UTILIZATION OF THREE-TRACK MAIN LINE

MOST OF these suburbanites are former automobile commuters who have kicked the driving habit and are ready to board the arriving GO train. The six month average for passenger volume through the early part of 1969 was as follows: Weekdays 16,100; Saturdays, 5,800; and Sundays, 2,900. Without the new train service, these people would have been on the highways adding to congestion that has drivers crawling instead of making any time or speed. (Courtesy Ontario Department of Highways)

PRIOR TO THE DELIVERY of the self propelled cars, the new GO Transit leased FP-7's and coaches from the Ontario Northland Railway to fill in. Here a push pull train meets a double ended ONR train (done to eliminate turning of ONR diesels at terminals.) on double track parallel to the Gardiner Expressway. (Courtesy Ontario Department of Highways)

FREE PARKING AND KISS-N-RIDE AREAS are provided at most of the GO suburban stations, such as this one at Oakville. (Courtesy Ontario Department of Highways)

The Grand Trunk Western

The State of Michigan has one of the finest highway systems in the United States. However, in the Detroit Area, the highway system is beginning to fail in doing its job of moving people. If more highways are built, the down town section will be sacrificed to parking ramps. The logical solution is rail service, and there are a number of lines radiating from Detroit on which a rail service could be provided. However, at the present time, there are only two railroads providing suburban service in Michigan. One company is the Grand Trunk Western.

The GTW operates 3 commuter trains each way on week days between Detroit and Pontiac, a distance of 26.3 miles. These trains provide morning and evening rush hour service to and from Detroit respectively. The morning trains are spaced 30 minutes apart arriving at Detroit from 7:30 A.M. to 8:30 A.M. The evening trains are also spaced 30 minutes apart departing Detroit from 5:00 P.M. to 6:00 P.M. On Friday evening, the last train departs 20 minutes later to give business men extra time to "wind things up" before the week-end. These week day trains handle over 2800 passengers. Incidently, the GTW experienced a 29.0% gain in patronage in 1968 over 1967. Needless to say, the GTW is quite happy with the new passengers that have "kicked" the driving habit.

Although, the GTW operates only 3 week day commuter trains in each direction, the service is supplemented by a Saturday morning and afternoon run to and from Detroit. This train and the week day commuters make all stops between Detroit and Pontiac.

In addition, week day and week end passengers can ride the Detroit-Durand Maple Leaf connection. This train leaves Detroit at 12:30 P.M. and stops at Milwaukee Jct., the Chrysler Plant, Royal Oak, Birmingham and Pontiac. The east bound run of the same train arrives at Pontiac at 5:03 P.M. and makes the above stops into Detroit. The week-day passenger therefore has a total of four trains in each direction to choose from.

One problem with commuter service is poor utilization of equipment. The GTW has the same problem, but the Company takes advantage of special events and holidays by providing extra service to the public at those times. There are two prime examples, the Thanksgiving Day Parade and the Christmas Season Shopper's Specials.

The GTW usually runs two Thanksgiving Day Special trains to down town Detroit's Santa Claus Parade. They start out from Pontiac. The trains leave Pontiac after 8 A.M. and make all intermediate suburban stops. Regular commuter fares and tickets apply. Upon arrival at Detroit, connecting Detroit buses take passengers to a spot near Campus Martius for a special 15 cent fare. After the parade, the trains depart Detroit, again making all suburban stops. The trains arrive in Pontiac in the early afternoon.

The GTW has operated Christmas Shopper's Spe-

cials for two years in a row now. These trains originate in Detroit and make two round trips (One in the morning and one in the afternoon) to Birmingham on a daily except Sunday Basis from the day after Thanksgiving through December 24th. These trains stop at Ferndale, Royal Oak and Oakwood Blvd. Commuter tickets are honored on these Shopper's Specials. In this way, the GTW is able to take at least some advantage of their equipment during idle periods of time.

Although the GTW's suburban operations are limited in scope, the service does provide a way for over 1400 people to be free of highway driving and parking worries. Hopefully the present GTW service is an embryo of a vast rail suburban service for the Detroit Area that will save lives and money on highway construction and maintenance costs.

THE GRAND TRUNK WESTERN RAILWAY was one of the last U.S. Roads to deselize their passenger service. Consequently, such streamlined power as 4-8-4 No. 6405 was often assigned to the commuter runs. Here the 6405 is departing Pontiac with a commuter train bound for Detroit in 1959. (Courtesy Bob Lorenz)

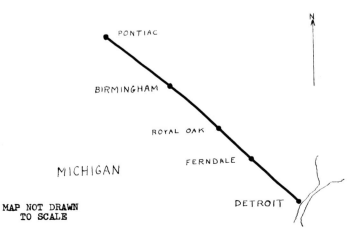

GRAND TRUNK WESTERN RAILROAD

DETROIT SUBURBAN TERRITORY

PONTIAC

BIRMINGHAM

ROYAL OAK

FERNDALE

MICHIGAN

DETROIT

MAP NOT DRAWN
TO SCALE

NORMAL STEAM POWER for Grand Trunk Western suburban trains and through trains on the Detroit-Durand run were these Class J, Pacifics. Here the 5629 is shown arriving at Pontiac with the overnight train from Chicago. This train has now been replaced by the fast evening train, the Mohawk. This photo was taken in 1958, when steam still handled GTW passenger trains. (Courtesy Bob Lorenz)

THE GRAND TRUNK WESTERN EMPLOYES GP-9'S on both their commuter and through trains. Brand new GP-9 (February, 1960) is on old No. 56 bound for Detroit at the Durand Station, Michigan. When the train reaches suburban territory at Pontiac, it will stop at Pontiac, Birmingham, Royal Oak and Milwaukee Jct. This procedure continues today (1969). (Courtesy S. K. Bolton, Jr., Rail Photo Service)

The Penn Central Company

The Penn Central also operates a suburban service west of Detroit. In this case, the territory extends from Detroit to Ann Arbor, a distance of 35.9 miles. The Company operates a daily except Saturday and Sunday rush hour train to Detroit in the morning, and to Ann Arbor in the evening. The two trains carry approximately 180 week day passengers.

At the present time, there are 3 westbound and 3 eastbound trains between Chicago and Detroit. One of these trains serves the suburb of Ypsilanti and all serve Ann Arbor. Although the service is not hourly, with the thru trains, the suburbanite has a fair amount of service to choose from.

The commuter trains are equipped with self propelled Rail Diesel Cars, and they provide the only all weather transportation west of Detroit.

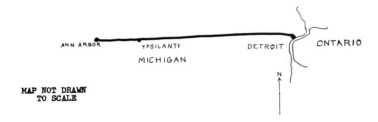

PENN CENTRAL COMPANY

DETROIT SUBURBAN TERRITORY

MAP NOT DRAWN
TO SCALE

THE PENN CENTRAL operates their Detroit suburban service with one Rail Diesel Car between Detroit and Ann Arbor. The car makes one round trip each day Monday through Friday. (Courtesy The Budd Company)

APPENDIX

Summary of Suburban Railroad Facts
By Size of Operation

1. *Long Island Railroad*
No. of Weekday Pass. 260,000
Suburban Mileage 334
Area Served New York City
Types of Tickets Sold: One Way
Round Trip
Weekly
Ten Ride
Monthly Restricted
Monthly Unrestricted

2. *Penn Central Company*
No. of Weekday Pass. 258,300
Suburban Mileage 722
Area Served Boston
New York City
Philadelphia
Detroit
Chicago
Types of Tickets Sold: One Way
Round Trip
Bargain One Way
10 Ride
Calendar Monthly

3. *Chicago & North Western Railway*
No. of Weekday Pass. 90,000
Suburban Mileage 178
Area Served Chicago
Types of Tickets Sold: One Way
Round Trip
25 Trip
Unlimited Weekly
Unlimited Semi-monthly
Unlimited Monthly
Flash Type

4. *Illinois Central Railroad*
No. of Weekday Pass. 78,000
Suburban Mileage 37
Area Served Chicago
Types of Tickets Sold: One Way
12 Ride Weekly
25 Ride
50 Ride Monthly

5. *Erie Lackawanna Railroad*
No. of Weekday Pass. 65,600
Suburban Mileage 307
Area Served New York City (Hoboken)
Cleveland
Types of Tickets Sold: One Way
One Day Round Trip
Round Trip
10 Ride
Weekly
Monthly

6. *Canadian National Railways*
No. of Weekday Pass. 49,000
Suburban Mileage 50
Area Served Montreal
Types of Tickets Sold: One Way
Unrestricted Monthly Flash

7. *Reading Company*
No. of Weekday Pass. 43,800
Suburban Mileage 159
Area Served Philadelphia
Types of Tickets Sold: Regular One Way
Regular 10 trip
Bargain One Way
Bargain 10 trip
Monthly

8. *Rock Island Railroad*
No. of Weekday Pass. 26,000
Suburban Mileage 46
Area Served Chicago
Types of Tickets Sold: One Way
Round Trip
Weekly
10 Ride
25 Ride
Monthly
Monthly School

9. *Boston and Maine Corporation*
No. of Weekday Pass. 24,000
Suburban Mileage 160
Area Served Boston
Types of Tickets Sold: One Way
12 Ride
Monthly
Flash

10. *Central Railroad of New Jersey*
No. of Weekday Pass. 24,000
Suburban Mileage 107
Area Served New York City (Newark)
Types of Tickets Sold: One Way
One Day Round Trip
Restricted Monthly
Unrestricted Monthly
12 Trip Weekly

11. *The Milwaukee Road*
No. of Weekday Pass. 22,000
Suburban Mileage 157
Area Served Chicago
Milwaukee
Types of Tickets Sold: One Way
Round Trip
10 Ride
25 Ride

Unrestricted Weekly
Unrestricted Semi-Monthly
Unrestricted Monthly
Flash

Unlimited Monthly
1000 Mile (Discontinued
1-1-68)

12. *Chicago, Burlington and Quincy*
  No. of Weekday Pass. 19,000
  Suburban Mileage   38
  Area Served   Chicago
  Types of Tickets Sold: One Way
                         Round Trip
                         10 Ride
                         25 Ride
                         Monthly Flash

16. *Southern Pacific Company*
  No. of Weekday Pass. 11,000
  Suburban Mileage   47
  Area Served   San Francisco
  Types of Tickets Sold: One Way
                         Round Trip
                         20 Ride Family
                         Weekly (7 day)
                         Monthly (5 Day)
                         Monthly (Every Day)

13. *Government of Ontario Transit*
  No. of Weekday Pass. 16,100
  Suburban Mileage   60
  Area Served   Toronto
  Types of Tickets Sold: One Way
  Ticket books are also sold for $5.00, $10,00 $15.00 and $20.00. The number of rides contained in each book depend upon the distance travelled.

  Tickets on GO are split into two portions, one surrendered on entry to station platform, and the other upon leaving the destination station. There are no ticket collections or sales made aboard trains. The separate ticket provides information on passenger movements and discourages unauthorized travel.

17. *Baltimore and Ohio Railroad*
  No. of Weekday Pass. 3,050
  Suburban Mileage   128
  Area Served   Baltimore
                         Washington, D. C.
                         Pittsburgh
  Types of Tickets Sold: One Way
                         Round Trip
                         10 Ride
                         12 Ride Weekly
                         Unlimited Use Weekly
                         Restricted Monthly
                         Unrestricted Monthly
                         46 Ride School 30 Day

18. *Grand Trunk Western*
  No. of Weekday Pass. 2,800
  Suburban Mileage   26
  Area Served   Detroit
  Types of Tickets Sold: One Way
                         10 Ride
                         46 Ride Monthly Flash

14. *Canadian Pacific Railway*
  No. of Weekday Pass. 16,000
  Suburban Mileage   109
  Area Served   Montreal
  Types of Tickets Sold: One Way
                         Round Trip
                         Various Multi-ride commutation

19. *Pennsylvania Reading Seashore Lines*
  No. of Weekday Pass. 700
  Suburban Mileage   156
  Area Served   Philadelphia
                         Camden
  Types of Tickets Sold: One Way
                         4 Day Round Trip
                         17 Day Round Trip
                         12 Trip Weekly
                         12 Trip Monthly
                         Restricted Monthly
                         Unrestricted Monthly
                         24 Trip (3 Months)
                         90 Trip (3 Months)

15. *Chicago, South Shore and South Bend Railroad*
  No. of Weekday Pass. 12,000
  Suburban Mileage   90
  Area Served   Chicago
  Types of Tickets Sold: One Way
                         Round Trip
                         10 Ride Bearer
                         25 Ride Bearer
                         25 Ride Family (Discontinued 12-31-60)
                         Limited Monthly

20. *Gulf, Mobile and Ohio Railroad*
  No. of Weekday Pass. Not Available
  Suburban Mileage   37
  Area Served   Chicago
  Types of Tickets Sold: One Way
                         Round Trip
                         Monthly

21. *Norfolk and Western Railway*

No. of Weekday Pass.	Not Available
Suburban Mileage	23
Area Served	Chicago
Types of Tickets Sold:	One Way
	Round Trip
	Monthly

22. *Pittsburgh & Lake Erie*

No. of Weekday Pass.	Not Available
Suburban Mileage	31
Area Served	Pittsburgh
Types of Tickets Sold:	One Way
	Round Trip
	Monthly

Above statistics are 1969 figures and were obtained from the various Public Relations Departments of the Suburban Railroad Companies.

Figure for Number of Weekday Passengers is amount carried in both directions. In other words, a passenger who travels from his home station to the Central City in the morning, and back again in the evening is counted twice.

Should the reader want more complete statistical information and the most recent data regarding the railroad commuter traffic, it can be obtained from the Annual Reports to the Stock Holders and to the Interstate Commerce Commission.

The following "Commuting Cost Comparison Chart" was designed by the Chicago & North Western Railway as one of the advertising techniques to lure motorists to the trains. The chart has been updated since its original publication. However, the reader should keep in mind that recent changes in automobile insurance rates and commutation fare increases will change the actual figures shown here slightly. A check of commutation fares of other railroads for a 40 mile round trip appeared to be fairly close to the fare shown here. Insurance rates for automobiles vary from area to area, even within a commutation district. However, it is felt by this writer, that the figures shown here will serve to point out that riding the suburban train is generally cheaper than driving your own car. The chart is provided Courtesy Chicago & North Western Railway.

>>>→

* Savings are even greater if the commuter walks to and from the station at both home and down town.

COMMUTING COST COMPARISON CHART
Based on typical daily 20 mile trip (40 mile round trip)

Automobile Commuting

	Typical Example

Gasoline
Multiply daily round-trip driving mileage by 243 working days a year (allows for 7 holidays and 2-week vacation). Divide annual mileage by average miles per gallon your car delivers and multiply by price you pay per gallon. (Add cost of any oil consumption between changes)
Example: 40 mi. × 243 days = 9,720 mi.
9,720 mi. ÷ 15 mpg. = 648.0 gals.
648.0 gals. × 30¢ (Regular Gas)
= 240.10   *34.9* $226.15 ~~$240.10~~

Tolls, if any
Example: 60¢ per day x 243 working days a year = $145.80   145.80

Parking Charges, if any
Example: 75¢ per day x 243 working days a year = $182.25   182.25

Service & Wear
Extra lubrication, oil changes, wear on tires and other parts, and repairs caused by commuting mileage
Example: 1¢ per mile x 9,720 miles = $97.20   97.20

Insurance
Increase in annual insurance premiums from Class 1A-o rate (car not used for commuting) to 1C-o rate (over 10 miles commuting)
Example: Increase in typical coverage for car in Chevrolet-Ford-Plymouth class, Mt. Prospect area

Bodily injury	$20.04
Property injury	7.00
Total Increase	$27.04

27.04

Depreciation
Note: Above figures are based on ownership of one car, with no depreciation charged. If automobile commuting requires you to own two cars, add to your commuting costs the full charges of annual insurance and depreciation of second car

TOTAL ANNUAL COST OF COMMUTING BY AUTOMOBILE   ~~$665.48~~   *678.45*

North Western Commuting

	Typical Example

Fare
Multiply cost of monthly unlimited ride ticket by 11 months, and add cost of one semi-monthly ticket (for vacation month)
Example: Average North Western commuter travels 20 miles. Using Mt. Prospect fare (20.1 miles), $24.00 x 11 + $13.42 = $277.55   *14.54   36.43* $305.27 ~~$277.55~~

Transportation to and from stations, if any
Between home and suburban station
Example: Wife drives commuter one mile to station in morning, returns home, picks him up at night. 4 miles per day × 243 working days = 972 miles per year. Using average gasoline cost (2.2¢ per mile) and service cost (1¢ per mile) from example shown above, 3.2¢ × 972 = 31.10   31.10*
Between Chicago terminal and office
Example: Typical commuter walks to and from office. 30¢ CTA shuttle buses also available to most Loop and Michigan Avenue locations. 30¢ × 243 = $72.90   *60¢*   *145.80* ~~72.90~~

TOTAL ANNUAL COST OF COMMUTING ON NORTH WESTERN   ~~$381.55~~   *482.17*

	Typical Example
Total Annual Savings When You Commute on North Western	*196.30* ~~$283.93~~

186

THERE ARE SEVERAL RAILROADS in the United States that do not operate commuter service or sell commutation tickets, but do have several trains that perform some of the same functions as commuter trains. For example, many through trains arrive in important cities early in the morning and depart in the late afternoon or evening. Such trains provide convenient service for shoppers, commuter businessmen and other one day travelers. Examples of such service operating today is Duluth-Minneapolis, Los Angeles-San Diego and many others. This photo shows a Santa Fe train that provided such service leaving Chicago en route to Los Angeles in the late afternoon during the days of steam. The locomotive is an oil burning Pacific No. 3448 heading up a standard consist of 10 cars. A passenger could even purchase a ticket for seat service in the Pullman cars. (Courtesy Santa Fe Railway)

THE **ONLY TRAIN** on the Santa Fe that arrives in Chicago early in the morning today is the "Texas Chief." The train arrives in Chicago shortly after 9:00 A.M., and departs Chicago after 5:00 P.M. The train is very convenient for people living beyond Joliet, Illinois. The "Texas Chief" is shown here prior to departure from Galveston, Texas. (Courtesy Santa Fe Railway)

THE **BALTIMORE & OHIO** provides a morning service to Chicago from Indiana points with its "Capital Limited." Equally good service returning is provided with the train's afternoon departure. The section of line between Chicago and Garrett is not a suburban district, but the trains have a number of regular passengers. As with many railroads, the B&O once operated several trains in each direction over their main line. This particular train is the now discontinued westbound "Diplomat," at Tiffin, Ohio, which provided afternoon service to Chicago. (Courtesy Bob Lorenz)

THE FORMER NORTHERN PACIFIC once operated a "North Coast Limited" connecting train between Duluth and Staples. Although in recent years the train ran with very few passengers, it was at one time patronized heavily by women traveling to Duluth for shopping. The train provided service to Duluth in the early morning, and departed in the early evening. Here was a case of too much competition by the automobile. The train died on May 25, 1969. The train is shown here departing Superior for Duluth with 4 passengers on May 17, 1969. In 1969, the one way fare on the train between Duluth and Superior was 25¢ as compared with 50¢ on the bus.

THE BURLINGTON NORTHERN operates a twice daily service in each direction between Duluth and Minneapolis-St. Paul. The trains, known as the Badger and the Gopher, provide excellent service for one day travel or business in either direction. This photo was taken in April, 1969 and is a Saturday morning version of the St. Paul bound Badger at Superior, Wisconsin.

AT ONE TIME, during the 1920's, the Soo Line Railroad was the big gun between Duluth and St. Paul-Minneapolis. The Road out did both the larger Great Northern and Northern Pacific with finer equipment and dining and library-observation cars. There were several trains in each direction that provided excellent businessmen commuter service. During that time, the Soo Line even published a book entitled, "When Sue Rode the Soo Line Between The Twin Cities and The Twin Ports." The depression killed most of the Soo Line service. From that time until the early 1960's, the Soo operated one round trip per day in a pool service with the Great Northern and the Northern Pacific. This photo shows how the Twin Ports-Twin Cities trains looked in the 1950's. The station is Duluth, Minnesota. (Courtesy Bob Lorenz)

INDEX

—A—
Abraham Lincoln, The: 149
Advertising Programs: 104
Aerotrains: 135
Alco Passenger Unit Type DL-109: 28
Aldene Plan: 55, 66
All Parlor Car Trains: 43
Ann Arbor, Michigan: 183
Atlantic City, New Jersey: 91
Atlantic Limited, The: 164
Ashland, Wisconsin: 11
Aurora, Illinois: 125, 128, 129
Automatic Ticket Collection: 137
Ayer, Massachusetts: 13

—B—
Back Bay Station: 22
Baltimore and Ohio R.R.: 22 to 26
Baltimore, Md.: 94 to 101
Bay Head Junction: 55, 56
Bayonne, N.J.: 66
Bedford, Mass.: 13
Bergen County Line: 60
Bi-level 400 Equipment: 114
Blue Island, Ill.: 131, 137
Boonton Line: 60
Boston and Albany R.R.: 22 to 26 also see
    Penn Central
Boston and Maine R R.: 13 to 22
Boston, Mass.: 8, 13 to 30
Boston North Station: 14, 15, 19
Boston South Station: 22
Brewster, N.Y.: 31
Broadway Limited, The: 154
Bryn Mawr, Pa.: 80
Budd Company: 60
Burlington Northern (See Burlington Route)
Burlington Route: 125 to 130

—C—
Canaan Branch: 33
Canadian National Railway: 168 to 174
Canadian Pacific Railway: 164 to 167
Cannon Ball, The: 43
Canton Viaduct: 29
Capital Limited: 94
Central Railroad of New Jersey: 66 to 73
Centralized Traffic Control: 126
Chestnut Hill, Pa.: 74, 80
Chicago: 103 to 154
Chicago and Eastern Illinois: 146
Chicago and North Western RY: 103 to 116
Chicago and North Western Station-Chicago:
    104
Chicago, South Shore and South Bend R.R.:
    144 to 147
Chicago Transit Authority: 6, 110, 138
Chicago Union Station: 117
Cleveland, Ohio: 102
Cleveland Union Terminal Electrics: 35
Club Cars: 40, 114
Clyburn, Ill.: 105
Coach Yards: 26, 58, 65, 70, 75, 111, 141
Coast Daylight: 163
Combination Baggage-Coach Cars: 18, 19,
    38, 39, 174
Combination Power-Coach Cars: 125
Commutation Passenger Miles: 11
Commutation Revenues: 11
Commuter 400: 114, 115
Connecticut Service: 31 to 41
Cos-Cab Station: 39
Crotan-Harmon: 36
Crusader, The: 79

—D—
Dearborn Station: 151
Dearfield, Ill.: 121
Del Monte, The: 159, 160
Delaware River Port Authority: 6
Detroit, Michigan: 180 to 183
Deux-Montagnes, Quebec: 168
Diner-Lounge Cars: 116, 145
Dining-Refreshment Car Service: 56
Double Deck Equipment: 48, 103, 112, 113,
120, 125, 141
Dover, N.J.: 60
Dual Powered Motive Power: 40

—E—
Elgin, Ill.: 118, 123
Elkhart, Ind.: 154
Empire Builder, The: 154
Equipment Utilization: 38
Erie Lackawanna Railroad: 60 to 65, 102
Erie Terminal: 62
Expressways: 9
Expressway Construction Costs: 10
Experimental Light Weights: 30, 135

—F—
Fan Trips: 38
Far Rockaway, Long Island: 42
Flatbush Ave.: 42
Foul Weather Friends: 101
"400" Streamliner: 114
"400" Streamliner Coach: 115
Framingham, Mass.: 22
Franklin, Mass.: 22
Freehold, N.J.: 68
Freight Service: 146

—G—
Gary, Indiana: 144, 145
Gas Electric Doodlebugs: 15, 85
General Electric Steeple Cab Electric: 32
General Steel Industries: 59, 83
Geneva, Ill.: 108
Glenside-Jenkintown: 74
Glenview, Ill.: 121
Government of Ontario Transit: 174 to 180
Grand Central Terminal: 31
Grand Trunk Western Railroad: 180 to 182
Greenport, Long Island: 42
Gulf, Mobile and Ohio Railroad: 147 to 150

—H—
Hamilton, Ontario: 175
Harpers Ferry, W.Va.: 98, 101
Harrisburg, Pa.: 80
Hartland, Wisconsin: 124
Harvard, Illinois: 108
Hatboro, Pa.: 74
Haverhill, Mass.: 13
Hawker Siddeley Self Propelled Coaches:
    174
Head-end Equipment: 41, 156
Hempstead, Long Island: 42
Hiawatha Coaches: 124
Highland, New Jersey: 70
Hinsdale, Ill.: 128
Hoboken Terminal: 65
Hunterspoint, Long Island: 42

—I—
Illinois Central Railroad: 137 to 143
Interior Passenger Equipment Photos: 19,
    50, 52, 59, 112, 113, 115, 116, 152, 162,
    176
Ipswich, Mass.: 13

—J—
Jamaica, Long Island: 42, 49
Jersey City, New Jersey: 70
Joliet, Illinois: 131, 150

—K—
Kenosha, Wisconsin: 108
Kiss-N-Ride Areas: 180

—L—
La Salle Street Station: 131, 132
Lake Geneva, Wisconsin: 108
Lansdale, Pa.: 74
Lark, The: 163
Lehigh Valley Railroad: 67
Lisle, Ill.: 129
Long Beach, Long Island: 42
Long Island Railroad: 42 to 54
Los Angeles, California: 11

Los Angeles Mail Train: 156
Louisville and Nashville Railroad: 11
Lounge Car Service: 104, 114
Lowell, Mass.: 13

—M—
Manayunk, Pa.: 80
Massachusetts Bay Transportation Authority:
    13, 14, 17
Massachusetts State Legislature: 14
Media, Pa.: 80
Merchants Limited: 30
Metroliners: 60
Metropolitan Transit Authority of Boston: 9
Metropolitans: 52, 53
Michigan City, Indiana: 144
Midday Congressional, The: 88
Milwaukee Road: 117 to 124
Milwaukee, Wisconsin: 114, 117
Missouri Pacific Railroad: 11
Montauk, Long Island: 42, 49
Montreal, Quebec: 164 to 174
Morristown, N.J.: 61
Motive Power Exchange: 56
Mount Royal Tunnel: 171

—N—
Naperville, Ill.: 129
National Limited: 101
Needham Branch: 26
Needham Heights: 22
New Brunswick, N.J.: 59
New England States, The: 22
New Hampshire: 18
New Haven, Conn.: 31
New Haven Railroad: See Penn Central, 22
    to 41
New Jersey: 54 to 73
New Jersey Proposed Improvements: 12
New Town, Pa.: 74
New York and Long Branch Railroad: 54 to
    57, 67 to 73
New York Central: See Penn Central
New York City: 31 to 73
New York, Susquehanna & Western Rail-
    road: 68
Newburyport, Mass.: 13
Non-stop Train Service: 25
Norfolk and Western Railway: 151 to 152
Norristown, Pa.: 74
Northbrook, Ill.: 122
Northeast Corridor: 34
Northwestern Pacific Railroad: 11

—O—
Oakland, California: 11
Omaha Railroad: 11
Ontario Northland Railway: 178
Open-end coaches: 126
Open-end Electric MU Equipment: 37
Orland Park, Ill.: 151
Ossining, New York: 36
Owl Faced Equipment: 48
Oyster Bay, Long Island: 42

—P—
Pacific Electric Railroad: 11
Panama Limited, The: 142
Paoli, Pa.: 80
Parlor Car Service: 43, 51, 89
Passenger Unloading and Loading: 161
Peninsula 400: 114
Penn Central Railroad: 22 to 41, 54 to 60,
    80 to 93, 153 to 154, 183
Penn Station: 43
Pennsylvania Railroad: See Penn Central
Pennsylvania Reading Seashore Lines: 91 to
    93
Philadelphia: 74 to 93
Pickering, Ontario: 175
Pittsburgh, Pa.: 94, 96, 100, 102
Pittsburgh and Lake Erie Railroad: 96, 102
Pontiac, Michigan: 181
Port-Authority Trans-Hudson (PATH) 60,
    66

Port Jefferson, Long Island: 42
Port Jervis: 61
Port Washington, Long Island: 42
Poughkeepsie, New York: 31, 36
Power Utilization Example: 28
Princeton, N.J.: 58
Providence, Rhode Island: 25
Pullman Standard: 50
Push Pull Trains: 71, 103, 108, 122, 130, 135, 136

—Q—

Quakertown, Pa.: 74

—R—

Rail Post Office Cars: 27, 41, 156
Railroad Equipment Costs: 10, 112, 160
Rapid Transit Systems: 8, 9, 104, 110
Raritan, N.J.: 66
Reading Company: 74 to 79
Reading Terminal: 74
Ricton, Ill.: 137
Rigaud, Quebec: 165
Rock Island Railroad: 131 to 136
Rockport, Mass.: 13
Roger Williams, The: 30
Route 128 Station: 27

—S—

San Francisco: 155 to 163

San Francisco Depot: 157
San Jose, California: 155
Smithtown, Long Island: 51
Snack and Beverage Service: 104
Snack Bars: 94, 100
South Amboy, N.J.: 56
South Bend, Indiana: 144
South Sudbury, Mass.: 13
Southeastern Pennsylvania Transportation Authority: 74 to 87
Southern Indiana Coal Mines: 11
Southern Pacific Company: 155 to 163
Speed Limits: 117
Spring Valley: 61
Springfield, Mass.: 24
State Government, New Jersey: 67
Staten Island Rapid Transit: 71
Stamford. Conn.: 33
Suffern: 60

—T—

Tavern Cars: 114
Thru Train Service: 17, 28, 30, 31, 32, 54, 74, 91, 126, 127, 174
Ticket Collection: 161
Toronto, Ontario: 174 to 180
Trenton, New Jersey: 54, 80
Turbine Cars: 42, 54
Tuxedo, The: 61

—U—

Urban Mass Transportation Act of 1964: 67

—V—

Valparaiso, Indiana: 153

—W—

Wabash Railroad: See Norfolk and Western Ry.
Walworth, Wisconsin: 118
Washburn, Wisconsin: 11
Washington, D.C.: 94 to 101
Wayne Junction: 75, 77
Week-ender, The: 43
West Chester, Pa.: 80
West Hempstead, Long Island: 42
West Trenton, Pa.: 74
Western Suffolk County, Long Island: 42
Westfield, New Jersey: 69
White Plains, New York: 35, 37, 40
Wilmington, Delaware: 80
Woburn, Mass.: 13
Worcester, Mass.: 22
World's Largest Tank Passenger Steam Locomotive: 23

—Z—

Zone Fare System: 137, 155